Connected

devotional readings for an intimate marriage

Willie and Elaine Oliver

Copyright © The Stanborough Press Ltd.
First published in 2020 by The Stanborough Press Ltd., Alma Park, Grantham, UK.

British Library Cataloguing in Publication Data. A catalogue record for this book is available from the British Library.

ISBN 978-1-78665-112-9

Designed by Abigail Murphy.
Cover design by David Bell.

Printed in India.

Dedication

To Jessica and Julian,
our beloved children.

The noblest gift we can give to you is our
unwavering love for God and for one another.

Introduction

Imagine if you could take your marriage up to the next level. What if it were possible to go from a relationship that survives to one that thrives? What if there were a way to strengthen your commitment to each other? What if better communication could create greater trust? And, best of all, what if grace could help you see the best in your spouse?

In *Connected: devotional readings for an intimate marriage*, Willie and Elaine Oliver share over 35 years of marriage experience, growing together, learning from each other, and rearing children. They know how to make the 'what ifs' become reality.

In their professional lives they serve as the Director and Associate Director of Family Ministries, respectively, for the General Conference of the Seventh-day Adventist Church. Willie is an ordained minister, a pastoral counsellor and a certified family life educator who holds Master's degrees in Religion and Sociology and a PhD in Sociology. Elaine is a licensed clinical professional counsellor and a certified family life educator who holds Master's degrees in Clinical Mental Health Counselling, Counselling Psychology, and Higher and Adult Education. She has completed coursework for a PhD in Educational Psychology. They are both adjunct professors of marriage and family at the Adventist University of Africa, and Willie also serves as an adjunct professor of family ministries at the Seventh-day Adventist Theological Seminary at Andrews University.

Their combined personal and professional reflections guarantee that what they share will not only be helpful, but inspire spouses to grow in their love and commitment to each other.

And just when you thought you'd heard this all before:

> 'Being married is always more than just being married
> if you are a follower of Jesus (or want to be).'

With 52 devotional reflections, there's a thought for each week of the year, specifically designed to help couples to pause (reflect on the ideas shared), pray (about the ideas shared and how they relate to their experience) and then choose (determine to experience change together). *Discover more by reading the next page to stay connected!*

Making It Good

**'And the Lᴏʀᴅ God said, "It is not good that man should be alone;
I will make him a helper comparable to him." '**
Genesis 2:18

What a remarkable God we serve! From the dawn of creation, He knew exactly how He wanted Planet Earth to look: flowers, plants, insects, birds, trees, dogs, giraffes, lions, tigers, bears, zebras, rivers, mountains, night, day, Sabbath, and much more. Humans, to be sure, have been made in His image, male and female, representing His plan for mutuality in marriage, family, relationships, and community.

God did not plan for humans to live in isolation: rather, to share complete communion with each other as husband and wife.

The Hebrew construction of the beginning of this verse gives prominence to the negative phrase, 'not good'. The picturesque environment God created for man was without doubt exquisite, magnificent, resplendent, and a spectacular space in which to live and work. Nevertheless, the parenthetic statement makes evident that the master plan God has in mind for the human race in Eden has not yet been realised.

Whether man felt alone as he became acquainted with the splendid visual extravaganza of creation is not recorded in Scripture. Only the divine perspective is shared. God means for humans to have fellowship with Him. Beyond that, however, God intends for us to have intimate relationships with each other. Essentially, man will not truly live until he loves and gives himself completely to another human being in total complementary commitment.

God did not plan for humans to live in isolation: rather, to share complete communion with each other as husband and wife. They were to reflect the image of God on earth, becoming the evidence of God's enduring love for His creatures.

One may, of course, love, give, and enjoy social relationships with others outside of marriage, and may completely fulfil God's plan for that person in doing so: some people are called to serve God as singles, and such a path is commended in Scripture (Matt. 19:10-12; 1 Cor. 7:7, 8, 32-35). Nevertheless, for most, marital union is the divine plan.

Ellen White elucidates the unfolding plan of God for the first couple when she writes: 'God Himself gave Adam a companion. He provided "an help meet for him" – a helper corresponding to him – one who was fitted to be his companion, and who could be one with him in love and sympathy' (*The Adventist Home*, p. 25).

As you navigate life with your spouse today, ask God to help both of you be the companions He intends you to be, and that the choices you make will keep you from feeling alone and isolated in the presence of each other. So your lives together may dramatise in significant and considerable ways the fulfilment and realisation of God's plan and intention: that of gifting human beings with the precious and treasurable experience marriage was created to be.

Pause

Reflect on this week's Bible text and devotional reading. Take turns sharing your thoughts in a kind and respectful manner.

Pray

Ask God to help both of you be the companions He intends you to be to each other, and that the choices you make will keep you from feeling alone and isolated in the presence of each other. Thank God for the gift of a suitable 'helper' and equal partner on the journey of life.

Choose

Choose one or two things you will do this week (individually and as a couple) to strengthen your companionship with each other:

....

....

....

....

....

....

....

....

....

....

....

....

....

Leaving and Cleaving

'Therefore a man shall leave his father and mother and be joined to his wife, and they shall become one flesh.' Genesis 2:24

Marriage establishes an entirely new entity of human reality. The truth is, the previous information in the text justifies the singular and distinctive relationship between man and woman: a connection uniquely strong and singular.

The introductory word, 'therefore', signals that the succeeding statement about the marriage of the man-woman pair communicates a worldwide responsibility, transcending all civilisations and epochs.

The development of the marital bond in this text is explained by employing three verbs, which denote three characteristics of marriage. The verb structure specifies God's intention for this unique relationship. The first verb, 'leave', infers the timelessness of this commitment: the man and the woman are now separated from their families of origin and are unable to go back to their initial state; their commitment to each other is meant to be forever. The second verb, 'be joined', proposes the unbroken nature of that relationship. And the third verb, 'become one flesh', indicates the deep, all-embracing, and profound quality of that relationship.

There is a need for healthy boundaries to be established between married couples and their parents immediately after the wedding.

Despite spending the formative time of our lives with

our parents or responsible adults, at marriage a new, all-encompassing reality becomes established and inaugurated for husband and wife. This is how God determined marriage should be from the very beginning. A lifelong commitment between a man and a woman is meant to convey the dedication, devotion, and allegiance that God declared should be operative between them from creation.

This indicates the need for healthy boundaries to be established between married couples and their parents immediately after the wedding, so that the sanctity of the new marriage may be appreciated. Such a decision would allow the newly established home the opportunity to be acknowledged as an entity separate from pre-existing relationships.

Has your marriage experienced the needed biblical injunction of leaving and cleaving? If this is not the case, what steps must you take to ensure and guarantee that such a transition takes place in the near future? When and how will you discuss this matter with your mate so that you are both on the same page about your need to leave and cleave?

Ask God for help today to be deliberate and kind in the process, so that you may accomplish your objectives and intentions without unduly hurting the relationship with both sets of parents.

Pause
Reflect on this week's Bible text and devotional reading. Gently and sensitively discuss what stage your marriage is at in this process.

Pray
Ask God to help you to be deliberate, patient, and kind in discussing 'leaving and cleaving'. Pray for wisdom during the process so that you may accomplish your objectives and intentions without unduly hurting your marriage or the relationship with both sets of parents.

Choose
Choose one or two things you will do this week (individually and as a couple) to set healthy boundaries for your marriage so you can experience 'leaving and cleaving'.

....

....

....

....

....

....

....

....

....

....

....

....

Naked and Not Ashamed

'And the man and his wife were both naked and were not ashamed.' Genesis 2:25 (ESVUK)

Our world is filled with shame. It is sin that has brought this shame, which comes from the guilt that emerges when we have done something other than what God made us to do.

 This biblical passage serves as a bridge to Genesis chapter 3, where the human race, represented by Adam and Eve, is about to suffer the consequences of shame brought on by the nakedness – embarrassment – that sin brings with it. It is the conclusion of the second creation story, analogous with the ending of the first creation story in Genesis 2:3.

The context of 'naked and ashamed' in Genesis 2:25 is a time of purity and joy experienced by the first couple: a time that has not yet been affected by sin. Their nakedness is connected to their oneness. Occupying a space of unity of thoughts, feelings, beliefs, goals and aspirations, agreement, closeness and affinity are what's being described here. It is what God chose for the first couple He married and tasked with being

'Naked and not ashamed' is genuinely a godly refrain that every married couple today should include, incorporate and embrace.

the ancestors of the human race. To be sure, it is still what God desires for every husband and wife today.

While we often think of 'naked and not ashamed' as

11

the introduction of sexual activity between Adam and Eve – the part all newly married couples are really interested in, and of course this is also true of many couples who have been married for many more years – the concept conveys much more than this.

'Naked and not ashamed' is genuinely a godly refrain that every married couple today should include, incorporate and embrace as a mantra to reclaim and live by: a birthright from the Creator Himself. Beyond the physical reality of nakedness – to be without covering or clothes – it denotes and connotes true intimacy between partners, where honesty, integrity, authenticity, reliability, openness and honour are operational in their transactions with one another every day.

This notion drives us to the reality of there being nothing to hide between spouses, and perhaps being practical about the way husbands and wives relate to each other every day about the very mundane substance of married life. In issues of money, spirituality, conversation, parenting, habits, and preferences, are you habitually naked and not ashamed when you relate to your spouse?

Ask God to help you have this experience today.

Pause

Reflect on this week's Bible text and devotional reading. Consider individually who you are when nobody is looking (even your spouse).

Pray

Ask God to help you and your spouse be open and transparent with each other.

Choose

What will you do this week (individually and as a couple) to enhance open and honest communication? Plan to find a good time to share, in a suitable location.

....

....

....

....

....

....

....

....

....

....

....

....

....

....

....

....

Let God Be the Architect

'Unless the Lord builds the house, those who build it labour in vain. Unless the Lord watches over the city, the watchman stays awake in vain.' Psalm 127:1 (ESVUK)

Several years ago, we built our first home. Well, to avoid any misunderstandings, we'll be clear that we didn't actually build the house with our own hands. Rather, we contracted professional builders to do so on our behalf.

The truth is, beyond knowing that we need to secure a plot of land, architectural plans, money or good credit to fund the project, and someone with expertise to execute the plans, we don't really know how to build a house. We may have a good idea about what we would like the final product to look like, but that is as far as we can go on our own.

We need Jesus.

The wise man, Solomon, in his second wisdom poem, deliberates about the question of launching into building a house, or constructing anything else for that matter, without God. He makes his point abundantly clear by proffering that any enterprise we pursue where God is not the protagonist is futile, meaningless and a waste of time, energy and resources.

Solomon further takes up this line of reasoning as the main premise of the book of Ecclesiastes, proposing the meaninglessness of earthly pursuits. In Ecclesiastes 1:2 he declares: 'All is vanity.' This, of course, is a way of philosophic discourse about the ultimate conundrum of life on earth.

Marriage, ladies and gentlemen, is no different. Since

we were all born in sin and shaped in iniquity –
referenced in Psalm 51:5 – ours is a very low probability
of success left to our own devices. Our default settings
from our families of origin in the best of circumstances
fall very short of the mark to make of marriage an
accomplishment worth sharing. We need Jesus.

Paul, the apostle, discovered the winning formula for
all things in the human ambit when he declared in
Philippians 2:5: 'Let this mind be in you which was also
in Christ Jesus.' Having the mind of Christ is what you
need to have a marriage filled with contentment and
peace. Unless God is the Architect of your marriage –
the One who understands the blueprint well, so every
feature of the construction is in the right place – your
building will soon crumble.

So, let Him be the architect of your marriage. Ask Him
to build your marriage today.

Pause

What did Paul mean when he said, 'Let this mind be in you which was also in Christ Jesus'?

Pray

Pray for a marriage relationship that is built on Christ; His selflessness, His mercy, His forgiveness, His kindness, and His gentleness.

Choose

Take one element of the character of Christ and practise modelling it with each other as many times as possible over the coming week.

....

....

....

....

....

....

....

....

....

....

....

....

....

....

....

Speak Softly

'A soft answer turns away wrath, but a harsh word stirs up anger.' Proverbs 15:1

No one enjoys being yelled at. The truth is, even people who enjoy yelling at others don't like to be yelled at. When pulled over by the police – even when one has completely disobeyed the law and driven 10 or 15 miles per hour above the speed limit – one does not appreciate it when the officer uses a tone of voice that has an edge to it, or is sardonic or contemptuous. Many may be thinking: 'Go ahead and give me a ticket if you want to; just allow me to keep my dignity intact.'

The book of Proverbs was written to help those who read it to be filled with wisdom and understanding. To be sure, it is a manual on wisdom, to help people learn to be prudent, careful and judicious as they negotiate relationships with others. Of course, one of the easiest mistakes to make in any relationship, but especially in very close and important relationships, is to say the right thing in the wrong tone; or, even worse, to say the improper thing in an unsuitable pitch.

Many quarrels develop not so much because the subject in question is that big a deal, but because of the attitudes people bring to the conflict.

Marriage is a relationship where we often say things we shouldn't to each other, and often do so in a harsh tone. The ability to prevent pointless bickering and to dwell in peace with others – especially one's spouse – is an asset of good sense and judgement. Many quarrels develop not so much because the subject in question is that big a deal, but because of the attitudes people bring to the conflict.

Think about the last time you and your spouse had a disagreement that became bigger than it really needed to be because of the way you responded. Were you more defensive than necessary, and perhaps more sensitive than the occasion demanded? Did you use offensive and loud language that exacerbated the situation, rather than employing a softer tone that could have abated the situation if your approach had been more conciliatory?

Regardless of what your pattern for responding has been, you can choose a wiser and kinder response in the days ahead. As you give careful attention to the scripture text for our deliberations today, may God help you and your spouse always to choose a soft and gentle response rather than a coarse and abrasive one, so that God will always be honoured in your relationship.

Pause

When have we reacted with harsh words to each other? Why did we react the way we did? Is it possible that some conversations we have are so difficult because the agenda is controlled by deep-rooted historic 'fears and threats' in our relationship?

Pray

Pray for the 'fears and threats' in the relationship. Ask the Lord for power to forgive each other of past 'issues' – and leave them with Him.

Choose

The apostle James instructs Christ-followers to be slow to speak and quick to listen (James 1:19). What a marvellous instruction to be applied as you communicate with each other! Is it worth practising this week?

....

....

....

....

....

....

....

....

....

....

....

....

Slow to Anger

'He who is slow to anger is better than the mighty, and he who rules his spirit than he who takes a city.' Proverbs 16:32

Dictionary.com defines anger as 'a strong feeling of displeasure and belligerence aroused by a wrong; wrath; ire'.

To be sure, anger is an emotion we can choose or refrain from selecting. Often we hear people say to another: 'You make me so mad!' – but is this so? Is anger really inevitable when someone says or does something to us that we don't like?

Google 'anger' and you will find a number of responses. The first one that popped up when we looked was from *Psychology Today*, which says: 'Anger is a corrosive emotion that can run off with a person's mental and physical health. Is holding it in the solution? Or letting it all out? Anger doesn't dissipate just because it is unleashed; in fact, that just rehearses it.' The statement further conjectures that, 'However raw it can be, anger is a necessary emotion, serves mankind well in certain situations, and, like all emotions, benefits from good management lest it cause self-harm or erupt into hostile, aggressive, or perhaps even violent behaviour towards others.'

Ultimately anger is harmful to the human body.

Often, there are philosophical postulations about anger: among them, that it is related to the 'fight, flight or freeze' response of the sympathetic nervous system. However, the fighting reference here doesn't necessarily mean throwing punches at another: rather, the impetus to battle against injustice, or poverty, or a disease that's ravaging a community.

Of course, psychological literature is loaded with evidence that the presence of anger is likely to compromise the viability of relationships. Ultimately it is harmful to the human body, since prolonged secretion of the stress hormones that appear with anger can devastate neurons in areas of the brain related to judgement and short-term memory. Also, anger is known for deteriorating the immune system.

The wise man Solomon is clear about the reality that anger needs to be managed and controlled, or it will become a destructive force that will hurt and easily damage relationships beyond repair.

If you find yourself having difficulty managing your anger, reach out to a Christian counsellor who works with an anger-management programme that could be helpful to you. Also, pray today and always that God will give you the capacity to control your anger; that by so doing you will avoid damaging your marriage and create a healthy environment in your home.

Pause

What are the 'pressure points' that cause me to be angry? Is such a response justified? Beside the potential for personal ill health, what physical and emotional health problems is it causing my spouse?

Pray

Reflect on the words of Proverbs 16:32. Pray for the Holy Spirit's power to be 'slow to anger'. If there have been times when you have 'lost control', pray for forgiveness from the Lord and from your spouse.

Choose

Choose together to communicate at a higher level if anger is a problem. Even if anger is not a problem in your relationship, why not do a check with each other on how you react to problems with each other and in general? Do you fight, flee or freeze?

....

....

....

....

....

....

....

....

....

....

....

....

Speak to Bless

'A word fitly spoken is like apples of gold in settings of silver.'
Proverbs 25:11

Whenever we read this passage of Scripture, the first thing that comes to mind is the concept of communicating with grace. Everyone who has ever been in a close relationship, especially a marriage relationship, has experienced impatience and even irritation, exasperation and annoyance when communicating with their spouse.

Communicating with grace conveys the idea of speaking to someone – in this case, one's spouse – in a way they may not deserve, since this is exactly the meaning of grace: 'unmerited favour', as the theologians tend to say.

The wisdom of Solomon is simply superb. When he references the notion of a word fitly spoken, what is being expressed is language that is appropriate for the occasion and for a specific person. Based on a person's temperament, what is heard by them can be different to what someone else hears; hence the wonderful characterisation by the wise man.

Just like gold and silver, your words can be received as a precious gift.

It is also fascinating to note the use of precious metals as a description of correct and appropriate words being spoken in a particular instance. While gold and silver are precious as gifts, when words are used appropriately, they are also very likely to be received as a precious present.

So we pose the question: how would you feel if, every time your spouse spoke to you, whatever he or she said and however he or she said it were like a gift of gold and silver? Would you like that? If you would like that, do you think your spouse would like it as well if you spoke to him or her in that same manner?

The truth is, if this were the reality of our daily interactions with our mate, we would be speaking to bless, because we would be mindful to express ourselves in affirming rather than invalidating ways, and in a respectful rather than a disrespectful manner. You would feel valued, and your spouse would feel appreciated, respected, and treasured as well.

Now, someone may be thinking: *You don't know my husband* or *You don't know my wife. S/he is so rude and obnoxious; I constantly feel the need to defend myself.* Well, if that is the case, we encourage you to embrace the message of this passage for your marriage today, and to determine to use words as if they were a gift of gold and silver so that you can communicate with grace and speak to bless.

Pause

The former preacher and evangelist John Stott defined 'grace' as 'love that stoops – and cares – and rescues'. Could this definition ably define your marriage?

Pray

Pray for 'the grace of the Lord Jesus Christ, and the love of God, and the communion of the Holy Spirit' to live and reign in you and your spouse (2 Corinthians 13:14).

Choose

'Grace' is more than a definition, a term or a concept: it is who Jesus is, the nature of His character! In what practical ways will you each seek to become more like Jesus in how you regard each other this week?

Trust Him Today

'You will keep him in perfect peace, whose mind is stayed on You, because he trusts in You.' Isaiah 26:3

Some time ago we were visiting a couple who had recently celebrated 20 years of marriage. The wife, who was still very excited about their recent vacation, shared with us: 'We just spent eight wonderful days in Santorini.'

It was obvious that she wanted us to know how much she and her husband cherished their marriage after two decades, and that it was a high priority for them to make the time and investment to celebrate this milestone in such a memorable way.

As soon as the wife mentioned the place of their vacation, the husband interjected, sounding almost upset: 'No, Mildred, it was MYKONOS, not Santorini, where we went. We only stopped in Santorini for 30 minutes on our way to Mykonos.'

Disrespectful and impolite correction can threaten our most significant relationships.

The body language of the very cheerful, confident, and pleased wife immediately changed to that of someone who had just been punched in the stomach. It became very evident that the once-beautiful day had become ominous, threatening, and filled with foreboding.

Unquestionably, Mildred was not trying to lie or misrepresent the facts about their anniversary vacation. She simply mixed up one beautiful Greek island with another; and, as helpful as the husband was trying to be, it merely underscored a distasteful sample of the affinity many of us have for correcting our mate in public. This also illustrates and exposes how disrespectful and impolite we often are, and by so doing we threaten our most intimate and significant relationships.

The attempted correction by the concerned husband was simply unnecessary, pointless, and uncalled for. Such an amendment added no real benefit to the wonderful conversation we were engaged in with this otherwise charming couple.

If you experience this kind of dialogue on a regular basis in your marriage – whether you play the role of the husband or the wife in this story – it is time to take stock of the injurious patterns of your interactions and decide to cut them out of your repertoire. Call on the Lord, who has promised to keep you in perfect peace if your mind is on Him and you trust in Him.

Ask for God's help to be thoughtful, kind, careful and considerate. As you invite God to fill you with His love and grace each day, you will develop patterns of communicating with your spouse that will be a blessing to your union and your witness for Jesus.

Pause

When have I put down my spouse, intentionally or unintentionally? Did I realise my pattern of poor behaviour? If necessary, have I apologised?

Pray

Pray for the power to elevate your spouse higher than yourself, through affirmation and support, in private, in the home and in the company of others.

Choose

Check to make sure that your marriage relationship is not governed by a 'me first' attitude. Try consciously this week to let your spouse 'go first' in as many practical daily activities as possible.

....

....

....

....

....

....

....

....

....

....

....

....

....

Have No Fear

*'Fear not, for I am with you; be not dismayed,
for I am your God. I will strengthen you, yes, I will help you,
I will uphold you with My righteous right hand.'* Isaiah 41:10

A dictionary definition of fear is 'a distressing emotion aroused by impending danger, evil, pain, etc., whether the threat is real or imagined; the feeling or condition of being afraid' (*dictionary.com*).

Fear is not an uncommon emotion experienced in marriage. Interestingly, it may show up early in the marriage, in mid-life, or even in the winter of life. Any number of circumstances may allow this sensation to surface, from feeling you married the wrong person after the first month of marriage has been a total disaster, to feeling disconnected, misunderstood and alone after 20 years of marriage, to being afraid you will lose your spouse to a debilitating illness after 40 or more years of enjoying a very high level of marital satisfaction.

Allow God's Word to replace the spirit of doubt, disbelief, misgiving and uncertainty.

Whatever is causing you fear or worry about your marriage, God is providing a message of optimism today. In fact, God is literally encouraging you not to allow anxiety to overwhelm you with pessimism and disappointment, regardless of the situation you are experiencing. To be sure, God is assuring you that His offer is not an empty and ordinary one. Rather, this pledge is based on God's righteous right hand. In other words, it is signalling God's almighty power, truth and reliability on your behalf.

So, if your fear is about thinking you married the wrong person, trust God to lead you to a pastor or Christian counsellor who is skilful at helping couples navigate difficult relationships and gain new perspectives and tools to take you the distance. Or, if yours has been a marriage that has brought more pain than joy, find a competent and God-fearing relationship professional who can help you reframe the trajectory of your marriage. Or, if it is the illness of your spouse that is causing apprehension, find new strength and comfort in reading God's Word and relying on spiritually strong friends to pray with you for healing or peace to grasp that God is always in control.

It is our prayer that you will allow the messages in God's Word to replace the spirit of doubt, disbelief, misgiving and uncertainty facilitated by the evil one; that, as you practise trusting the promises of God, your perspective will be transformed to allow you to enjoy the peace God wants you to have today in your marriage.

Pause

When it comes to life and family matters, what really frightens me? What frightens us? Gently share together those fears in a supportive and understanding way. More listening may be required than speaking by either spouse.

Pray

Pray for those very fears. Place them before the Lord, and give them to Him. Let Him take control of them, first to give you promised peace, and then to work with you in finding a solution or resolution – in His time.

Choose

This week, read Scripture together, and focus on the promises of God. Passages that come quickly to mind are Romans 8:28-39; Psalm 23; Jeremiah 31; and 1 Corinthians 10:13.

Be Wise Today

*'Therefore whoever hears these sayings of Mine, and does them,
I will liken him to a wise man who built his house on the rock:
and the rain descended, the floods came, and the winds blew
and beat on that house; and it did not fall, for it was founded on
the rock. But everyone who hears these sayings
of Mine, and does not do them, will be like a foolish man
who built his house on the sand: and the rain descended,
the floods came, and the winds blew and beat on that house;
and it fell. And great was its fall.* Matthew 7:24-27

While there are no perfect marriages (because there
are no perfect people), some marriages are stronger and
healthier than others because of choices made by each
of the partners every day.

Our text for today comes from the Sermon on the
Mount, the title frequently used for the teachings of
Jesus found in Matthew chapters 5-7.
These teachings were delivered by
Jesus to His disciples and others
interested in living a life in harmony
with God's principles. Although the
story is actually a metaphor about how
we should live our lives, the message is
clear. To have a successful outcome in
anything we do, especially in spiritual
matters, of which marriage is one, we
must obey God.

Build your marriage on the principles of patience and kindness.

Obeying God means building on the rock. Disobeying
God's directives means building on the sand. Of course,
what's right and what's wrong are often up for grabs in
the postmodern world we inhabit today. Still, the
message of Jesus is that simply hearing what He is

teaching isn't enough. Having a solid foundation only becomes a reality when people do what Jesus says about how we should live.

Among the teachings of Jesus directed at marriage in the context of the Sermon on the Mount are: a) not committing adultery and lusting for someone who is not your spouse (Matt. 5:27, 28), and b) not divorcing your spouse except for sexual immorality (Matt. 5:32); so following these two teachings would certainly indicate building your marriage on the rock, to aid in having a marriage that goes the distance.

Today we encourage you to build your marriage on the principles of patience and kindness found in 1 Corinthians 13:4. This will make your home the kind of place where strong and healthy relationships are viable through the presence and power of God.

Pause

As husband and wife, how seriously do we take the teachings of Jesus as outlined in His Sermon on the Mount? During His teaching, Jesus said a number of times, 'You have heard it said, . . . but I say to you. . . .' Previously we considered the matter of getting angry. In this sermon Jesus puts 'anger' on a par with murder, and 'looking at a woman lustfully' on a par with adultery.

Pray

Meditate on the words of 1 Corinthians 13:4, 5. 'Love is patient and kind; love does not envy or boast; it is not arrogant or rude' (ESVUK). Pray for the Lord to lead you and your spouse to understand what it really means to love as He loved.

Choose

Seeking to live patiently and kindly this week, does your spouse have a persistent habit that irritates? No matter how much you encourage and request change, the habit persists. At the stage where the spouse is weary of you 'going on' about it, and has 'shut down' at your nagging, what would happen if, instead of 'nagging', you tried a different method? What if you went the extra mile to be 'kind'?

....

....

....

....

....

....

....

....

Stay Together

'So then, they are no longer two but one flesh. Therefore what God has joined together, let not man separate.' Matthew 19:6

Marriage is God's idea. It was He who declared in Genesis 2:18, 'It is not good that man should be alone; I will make him a helper comparable to him.' Still, we have met many couples around the world who cannot wait to be separated or divorced from each other.

Often, we think about marriage as a bird cage. Those on the outside can't wait to break in, while those on the inside can't wait to break out. But, really, what is it that makes people rush to get married after having met only a few days or weeks before? And why is marriage sometimes approached like a sale at an exclusive department store that will only last a few hours or days, and you simply can't afford to miss out on the deals?

Everything that is a meaningful accomplishment takes effort, patience and dedication.

Clearly, marriage is meant to be taken seriously and entered into only after careful and prayerful consideration; and, given that marriage is the foundation of stable families, and families are the basis of society, the more stability there is in families, the healthier and happier they will be. This means that when you have strong and healthy marriages, you are more likely to have strong and healthy families, churches, communities, and countries. Truly, everything that is a meaningful accomplishment takes effort, patience and dedication: which is certainly the case with marriage.

No wonder God put very detailed and demanding parameters in place when He designed marriage. He knew we would have a penchant for wanting to get out at the first sign of trouble and run away, rather than being more considerate, introspective, thoughtful, empathetic and unselfish. In the words of a Hollywood actor and leading man who had been married to his wife for many years, when asked in a television interview how he had been able to remain married for so long, he declared: 'Not having divorce as an option in our marriage.' He concluded by saying: 'Marriage is so challenging that if divorce were an option, we would have taken it a long time ago.'

What we know, after 30-plus years of marriage and studying marriage for several decades, is that when both partners are thoughtful, committed, and include God in their marriage each day, any marriage can be saved if the husband and wife both want it. So pray for your marriage today, and trust God to help you make it good.

Pause

Talk together about marriage as ordained by God to be 'permanent' and 'exclusive'. What does that mean, and why has God made it that way? Some feel it to be a burden; others, a blessing. How do you both feel?

Pray

Thank God for the blessings you've already both received as a result of your commitment to each other before God, whether together for 1, 5, 10, 25, or even 50+ years.

Choose

Perhaps a married couple you know are going through difficulties at present. Without in any way interfering in their situation without being invited, and where they've made you aware of their struggle, in addition to making their situation a matter of prayer, think of some practical ideas of ways to help them that might ease the pressure points in their relationship.

Count the Cost

'For which of you, intending to build a tower,
does not sit down first and count the cost,
whether he has enough to finish it?' Luke 14:28

To have a marriage that will remain healthy and strong, begin with the end in mind. That is one of the things that can be inferred from this verse of Scripture. And, while the primary application of this passage is about seriously considering the cost of discipleship – what it takes to follow Jesus – marriage is fundamentally the same, at least in this respect.

Here we are not speaking about money. Rather, we are communicating about the importance of being intentional regarding the components needed to build the fabric of a marriage that will give you an enduring and resilient relationship.

We like to think of the journey of marriage as the flight of an aeroplane. How so, you may ask? Well, every time an aeroplane goes from point A to point B – let's say from London to Paris – there are three primary features that are a part of that reality:

1. There is a clear destination in mind;
2. The pilot has to file a flight plan; and
3. The pilot has access to a compass.

It is important to have a guide that is reliable to lead you.

During this flight there are winds and storms that may force the pilot to fly higher, or to go east, or west. However, because there is a clear destination in mind, a flight plan, and a compass, the flight almost always arrives at the correct destination near the time expected.

Similarly, for marriage to be viable, you must: 1. Have a clear destination in mind; 2. Be deliberate about what is in your flight plan and what is left out of it. Your flight plan includes the values that fuel the vehicle of your marriage. Among these values should be patience, kindness, honesty, commitment, fidelity, respect, love, joy, your relationship with God, and many other virtues. Undeniably, to be successful in marriage, what you leave out of your flight plan is just as important as what you include. Elements like criticism, contempt, defensiveness, dishonesty, infidelity, violence and other unsavoury values should be categorically left out of your flight plan. And, last but not least, 3. Have a compass (the Bible). Since there are so many opinions about marriage in society, it is important to have a guide that is reliable to lead you the right way. Like the flight of an aeroplane, you may run into storms and winds that will take your marriage off course, but by following the compass – the Bible – your marriage will travel to the destination of commitment and happiness where God wants it to go.

It is our prayer that when it comes to your marriage you will begin with the end in mind.

Pause

It is true to say that a value is only important to us if we practise it. For example, many Christians will say that 'prayer' is an important value they hold. But do they pray? What are the three top values you share together in your marriage?

Pray

Pray for the values you share to be grounded in God's Word, to be able to reflect His character not only to each other, but also to children, parents and extended family members, and the list keeps going on and on. . . . Thank God for the example of Jesus, who shows us how to live.

Choose

Go on a Bible hunt this week to discover the values it speaks about. The most obvious place to start is 1 Corinthians 13; but don't stop there, as Paul's letters, full of 'instruction', are grounded in values. What about the life and teachings of Christ? How did His actions reflect His teachings?

....

....

....

....

....

....

....

....

....

....

Because of Your Love

'By this all will know that you are My disciples, if you have love for one another.' John 13:35

Being married is always more than just being married if you are a follower of Jesus (or want to be). After all, we are not truly disciples unless we understand the responsibility that goes along with that designation.

The Good News Bible presents it this way in Matthew 5:14, 16: 'You are like light for the whole world. A city built on a hill cannot be hidden. . . . In the same way your light must shine before people, so that they will see the good things you do and praise your Father in heaven.'

Of course, the metaphor of being light is often misunderstood as trying to be a show-off or trying to bring attention to yourself, which is not what this is about. Rather, living by the values of Jesus our Lord means leading a life of humility, kindness, patience, peace, and gentleness, which cannot be hidden in our society today.

Loving your spouse like Jesus will identify you as a follower of Christ.

This kind of existence will get you noticed without a doubt. In fact, this is what Jesus is sharing with His audience in Matthew's account of the Sermon on the Mount, as a way to live a life devoted to the values of the Kingdom of God. To be sure, it is the essence of our lead verse for today. If you are a husband or a wife who embraces these ideals, you will create a desirable home environment that people around you will want to emulate. More than that, you will be like a light that shines into the darkness that so many are experiencing in their marriage relationships today.

What John suggests is that if you love like Jesus wants you to love – and here we are specifically talking about loving your spouse – that kind of loving will identify you as a person who is a follower of Jesus; and this reality will lead people around you to want to glorify the God who causes this kind of relationship.

So your marriage is not only to advantage your life and that of your spouse and children. It is also to be a catalyst for joy, peace, patience and healthy relationships with those in your circle of influence. Allow God to use your marriage relationship in this way today, and stimulate a growing reality of healthy relationships until Jesus returns.

Pause

What effect has your commitment to and love for each other had on your children?

Pray

Thank God – again – for your stable and growing relationship – centred 'in Him' – that has the potential to be an example to others. Pray that the deep-rooted and committed love you have for each other will be a tremendous example not just in the family, but also in the community.

Choose

Love is the most misunderstood word in the English language. Often understood to focus on sentimental, self-centred feelings, are there ways in which, working together, you can create teachable moments for your children (even if they are now adults) when you show them that true love goes much deeper than feelings? While feelings are important, they are not the litmus test of love. Can you think of examples in your marriage where you have gladly put the needs of your spouse before your own?

Peace Indeed

'Peace I leave with you, My peace I give to you; not as the world gives do I give to you. Let not your heart be troubled, neither let it be afraid.' John 14:27

Peace is a fascinating concept that may raise different perspectives in people depending on who they are, where they live, and what they have experienced. If we search Wikipedia it will tell us, 'Peace is a concept of societal friendship and harmony in the absence of hostility and violence.' It goes on to share: 'In a social sense, peace is commonly used to mean a lack of conflict (such as war) and freedom from fear of violence between individuals or groups.'

Where the Spirit of the Lord is, there is peace, understanding and hope.

We have encountered other descriptions of the same word, like 'freedom from disturbance; tranquillity'; also, 'a state or period in which there is no war or a war has ended'. It may also be used as an informal greeting in the United States by simply stating, 'Peace'; or as an informal saying to indicate leaving, like the verb: 'I peaced out.'

In John 14 we find Jesus with His disciples at a time of His departure, just before going back to His Father. While 'Peace' was an established Jewish greeting and farewell in New Testament times, Jesus is doing much more than saying hello or goodbye to His disciples. Jesus reassures the 12 throughout the chapter; verse 27, though, is the heart of His message of peace. This peace, to be sure, is different to the ordinary peace humans conceptualise as the absence of war, hostility, or conflict. Here, peace means more than simply the absence of confrontation or disagreement. In fact, it isn't so much suggesting the lack of trouble as indicating the presence of the Spirit of God.

If you've been married for more than a month you are already conscious that controversy is inevitable in marriage, because it is often made up of two very different individuals who are in love with their own opinions. This divergence of thought brings with it a measure of anguish, agony, distress, misery and sorrow. Nevertheless, the promise of peace Jesus made to His disciples is also ours today. Despite the dissimilarities you may have with your spouse, Jesus promises the presence of His Spirit: and where the Spirit of the Lord is, there is peace, understanding and hope.

Embrace this reality in your marriage today, and experience the peace God wants you to have.

Pause

A peacekeeper is someone who wants to keep the peace by avoiding conflict.

A peacemaker is someone who wants to resolve conflict in order to create peace.

In your marriage, are you peacekeeping or peacemaking?

Pray

Pray for the peace of God which is beyond human understanding – but is promised (Philippians 4:7), which means experiencing the presence of God in all circumstances.

Choose

This week, wherever possible, if difficulties arise between you, pledge to try and resolve conflict to create peace.

You Can Trust Him

*'And we know that all things work together for good
to those who love God, to those who are the called
according to His purpose.'* Romans 8:28

God blessed you with your marriage because of His deep desire to see you saved in His Kingdom. How so, you may ask? Well, each time you disagree about something and find a way to patch things up, God is teaching you patience and forgiveness, helping you to grow into your best self. And every time you or your spouse are challenged by illness, an important need, or a disappointment, you get an opportunity to exercise your faith, which behaves just like a muscle. The more you get to work it, the stronger and more robust it becomes.

After more than three decades of being married to each other and working together to help couples develop a stronger and healthier marriage, we have learned that magnificent marriages are built over time, rather than put together instantly. They are like a four- or five-course gourmet meal with exquisite and exotic flavours that emerge over hours of careful and meticulous preparation, instead of a TV dinner prepared by microwave in 60 seconds.

The more you get to work your faith, the stronger and more robust it becomes.

So, the other day I (Willie) went for my customary three-mile (5K) early-morning run as a favour to my body, in order to remain as healthy and strong as possible given our taxing work and travel schedule. Upon returning from my run, I returned to our bedroom to take a shower and head to the office for meetings. I immediately noticed that Elaine was already out of bed, yet the bed was still unmade. Feeling a bit frustrated, I walked to the door of our bedroom and called for Elaine – I knew she was in the house somewhere, probably having her personal time with God. 'Babe!' I yelled. Sensing my disposition, Elaine answered cautiously: 'Yeees?' I continued, 'Do you think you can make the bed when you are the last one to get out of it?' Slowly, and in a measured tone, Elaine responded, 'Sure.'

When I had showered and was ready to begin my day, Elaine was now in our bedroom, evidently with more to say. 'Sweetheart,' she mused, 'you think that after all the years we've been married, when you find our bed unmade, you can just make it?' My jaw tightened, but, rather than countering reactively, the Spirit of God spoke through me as I answered sincerely, 'Yes, I can.'

This is a reminder that God is still working things out for our good, and we can trust Him. We are being polished in the workshop of marriage, preparing us to live with Jesus forever.

Pause

It is relatively easy to show grace, mercy and kindness to those we meet in the market place, in business, in college, and in church. But 'would you be as patient as I am with . . . ? You don't live with them!' Share together, in a grace-filled and gentle manner, the things in your domestic life that tend to wind you up.

Pray

Lord, help us both to be selfless rather than selfish. Help us to grow in faith and spiritual maturity so that, whatever life challenge we face, we may draw closer to You, claiming both Your presence and Your love.

Choose

Surprise each other this week by role-reversing some domestic chores. At the very least, it will cause each of you to smile!

Boundless Love

*'Who shall separate us from the love of Christ? Shall tribulation,
or distress, or persecution, or famine, or nakedness, or peril, or
sword? As it is written: "For Your sake we are killed all day long;
We are accounted as sheep for the slaughter."
Yet in all these things we are more than conquerors
through Him who loved us.'* Romans 8:35-37

We have always disliked being away from each other
for any number of days. Even now that we work
together, travel together, and seem not to have any time
away from each other, we still have a distaste for being
separated from each other for too long.

Perhaps right about now someone may be thinking,
'Spouses need time away from each other every so often
just to get an opportunity to breathe and live without
being criticised or bothered.' While this might be true,
for relationships to grow together, especially marriage,
spouses need to be together, even to practise new
relational skills together, to keep their marriage
relationship viable.

*What choices
are stopping
your relationship
with God?*

Sometimes, in our relationship with
Christ, we become so absorbed with all
sorts of issues in life that we have no
time for Him. The truth is, before we
know it, we have drifted from
meaningful connection with Him: His
absence being evident by the
deterioration of our relationships,
especially the relationship with our
spouse.

What are you doing these days that is keeping you
from having an optimal relationship with Jesus? Is it

preoccupation with your work that is keeping you from Jesus? Is it juggling marriage, parenting, volunteering, and doing other good things that is keeping you from having time with Jesus? Or do you find yourself engaged in wasteful and mundane activities like an obsession with YouTube clips, or FOMO (Fear Of Missing Out) that keeps you glued to all your social media platforms?

What choices are you making that are stopping you from having a meaningful relationship with God?

A prevalent concept in Judaism was that suffering embodied being under the curse of God. Essentially, it was seen as a symbol of God's disapproval of a person. In our meditation for today, Paul is actually repeating the message of Romans 8:1, that there is no condemnation for those who are in Christ Jesus, even if suffering is present in their lives.

Our prayer for you today is that, regardless of whatever burden or hardship you may be experiencing – even if it has to do with your marriage or family – you will know that God is with you every step of the way.

Choose to spend quality time with Jesus today, so that your existence will be filled with His peace, grace and love.

Pause

Choose to spend quality time with Jesus today, so that your existence will be filled with His peace, grace and love.

Pray

'Keep your wants, your joys, your sorrows, your cares, and your fears before God. You cannot burden Him; you cannot weary Him' (Ellen G. White, Steps to Christ, *page 100).*

Choose

If possible, get hold of the book Steps to Christ, *or read it online, and read together as a devotional activity the chapter on 'The Privilege of Prayer'.* https://m.egwwritings.org/en/book/108/toc

Do the Right Thing

'Let love be without hypocrisy. Abhor what is evil. Cling to what is good. Be kindly affectionate to one another with brotherly love, in honor giving preference to one another.' Romans 12:9, 10

From time to time, despite working together on behalf of stronger and healthier marriages and families around the world, we find ourselves displeased with each other. Sometimes this happens at the most inopportune times: for example, just after arriving at a beautiful vacation spot God has blessed us with to have some down time and reconnect with each other. We find that it is very easy to say the wrong thing at such a time, annoying the other person no end.

Have you had a similar experience? If you have, you can easily relate to what we are saying. If you haven't, you'll soon have an occasion to do so, since having a strong and healthy marriage is not a destination. What we mean is that the healthiest of marriages are still between imperfect human beings who invariably behave very humanly and irritate each other; and the thing we say is not really said to exasperate our mate on purpose: we simply say it without thinking.

Marriage was designed to be a blessing and to reflect God.

The truth is, whether we are aware of it or not, we are involved in the great controversy: the battle between good and evil; the combat between Jesus and Satan. And marriage – being the first institution established by God at creation, which He called very good, designed to be a

53

blessing to humankind and to represent the image of God – is often where this battle is raging. To be sure, this is on purpose, for the reason that every time Satan can turn into a curse what God meant for a blessing gives him points in the battle that is being fought between good and evil: and our destiny is at stake.

Paul's message in today's text for meditation, then, is that we must be intentional each day about who and what we are living for. We cannot afford to begin our day without having our minds made up from the very outset about whom we belong to and how we will rely on His power and grace to represent Him well in all we do or say.

So, pray today for God's love, joy, patience and peace to fill your soul. Since being filled with God's Spirit is the only sure way to love without hypocrisy, cling to what is good; be kind; be affectionate; and be deliberate about speaking kind words to your mate.

Pause

Do negative thoughts sometimes dominate your thinking – for whatever reason? Could it be that regularly reading Scripture helps lift the spirit and serves as an antiseptic to what has become a habit? Talk together about this matter.

Pray

There's an old song which is really a prayer: 'Into my heart, into my heart, come into my heart, Lord Jesus. Come in today; come in to stay.' Its sentiments concur with the invitation given in Revelation 3:20.

Choose

Together, determine that in all matters this week – the mundane, the joyful and the serious – your decisions will be Christlike.

Celebrate Each Other

**'Do not deprive one another except with consent for a time,
that you may give yourselves to fasting and prayer;
and come together again so that Satan does not tempt you
because of your lack of self-control.'** 1 Corinthians 7:5

God created marriage with many reasons and purposes in mind. Intimacy, for sure, was one of God's principal reasons for gifting humans with marriage. Contrary to the belief of many that sexual relations in marriage are a necessary evil, they are God's distinct present to those who have chosen the extraordinary commitment of marriage.

The gift of sexual relations cannot be appropriated, demanded, seized, taken or grabbed.

In Genesis 2:24, 25, immediately after the pronouncements made by Adam when God brought Eve to him to unite them in marriage, there is a remarkable declaration that characterises marriage: 'Therefore a man shall leave his father and mother and be joined to his wife, and they shall become one flesh. And they were both naked, the man and his wife, and were not ashamed.'

The 'becoming one flesh' and 'being naked and not ashamed' are a revelation of God's recipe for remaining close to each other in a way no other human relationship could or should be. This 'one flesh' experience connotes mutuality, empathy, support, affinity and reciprocity in all areas of life; and the 'being naked and not ashamed' is emblematic of a blessing to be enjoyed, relished, appreciated and delighted in without fear, reservation, hang-ups, shyness or self-consciousness.

This gift of sexual relations with one spouse is exactly that: a precious gift. It cannot be appropriated, demanded, seized, taken or grabbed. It is shared among equals who have nurtured their marriage to be a place of affection, tenderness, kindness, friendliness, warmth, love and passion.

In writing to the Corinthians, the inhabitants of a city where sexual relationships had become perverted, degraded and immoral, Paul is helping the Corinthians to reframe God's original intention. A gift so precious, meant to keep marriage connected, united and bonded, cannot be disregarded or kept from each other for too long, especially without mutual consent.

It is our prayer that you will take Paul's counsel to heart; that you and your spouse will do all you can, each day, to create an environment of sweetness and warmth in your marriage. This will put you in a frame of mind to want to celebrate God's wonderful gift on a regular basis with each other. And, last but not least, you will reap the benefits of protection from temptation and be the recipients of a marriage that gives honour and glory to God each day.

Pause

Is it easy or difficult to talk with each other about 'intimacy'? Is there any other single matter in marriage that requires each spouse to show respect and put the other first? Check to ensure that each of you has the emotional maturity to discuss this in an appropriate and sensitive way.

Pray

Pray for the Lord to give you both mutual patience and understanding of each other. Pray most of all for the gift of patience.

Choose

Problems with 'intimacy' in marriage can sometimes be long-term, and may have arisen as the result of past negative experiences prior to marriage. It may be appropriate to seek counselling from a certified marriage counsellor or medical doctor.

....

....

....

....

....

....

....

....

....

....

A Way of Escape

'No temptation has overtaken you except such as is common to man; but God is faithful, who will not allow you to be tempted beyond what you are able, but with the temptation will also make the way of escape, that you may be able to bear it.'
1 Corinthians 10:13

Temptation is defined by *Dictionary.com* as 'the act of tempting; enticement or allurement'. An additional meaning offered is 'the fact or state of being tempted, especially to evil'. The same source describes escape as 'to slip away from pursuit or peril; avoid capture, punishment, or any threatened evil'; also 'to succeed in avoiding (any threatened or possible danger or evil)'.

Quite frequently, persons with power as well as persons with very little power get caught in ethical breaches having to do with money or an illicit relationship. What's really intriguing is that, with so many getting caught, you would think that others would be dissuaded from making the same mistakes. Nonetheless, this is not the case. Every year you can count on more individuals getting snared, with devastating results for themselves and their families.

The truth is, everyone is human, and every human is filled with shortcomings.

As you already know, many marriages end in divorce each year, and not a few terminate much more unfavourably than that because of poor choices made by one or both of the spouses. A habit many couples allow themselves to indulge in is the fantasy of being with someone other than their spouse who might be prettier and younger, or taller and wealthier. More often than not, the reality is nowhere close to the fantasy and is terribly disappointing. The truth is, everyone is human, and every human is filled with shortcomings and idiosyncrasies that are often much more dangerous and serious than what we were experiencing with our spouse.

The context of our scriptural meditation for today finds Paul retelling the story of the children of Israel's deliverance from Egyptian bondage and the subsequent destruction of many of the Israelites because of their disobedience. Essentially, the message for married couples today is that there is no reason to go down the road many have already travelled with grave consequences. By the grace of God, because of the choices you will make today, your story will have a different ending. We pray that you will always bear in mind that in the middle of every temptation God is present to offer you His strength and the victory if you obey.

Pause

Talk together about the blessings of the marriage vow being permanent and exclusive. Is there a reason, or many reasons, why God made it that way?

Pray

'And do not lead [either of] us into temptation' (Matthew 6:13). What does it mean to keep your eyes fixed on Jesus (Hebrews 12:2)?

Choose

How the media portrays relationships, and marriage in particular, is far from God's design. Not only that, but more often than not it glamorises the alternative. Is it possible to be influenced by what we see? Talk together about what you watch, read and see, and see if there is room for improvement.

Good Fruit

'But the fruit of the Spirit is love, joy, peace, longsuffering, kindness, goodness, faithfulness, gentleness, self-control. Against such there is no law.' Galatians 5:22, 23

Love of any kind exists because the person doing the loving has made a choice to love. This notion of love, truly, is much more than being romantically in love with someone you dream about spending the remainder of your life with.

Some time ago, a friend shared a story about a mutual friend who was single and seemed to enjoy the attention of her church family. To be sure, one of the challenges of being a single adult in church – whether man or woman – is having to navigate the minefield of quite a number of persons volunteering to find you a love interest or life partner. People often believe that if an individual is not romantically involved with someone else, they most likely lead a lonely, gloomy, miserable and bleak existence; so finding them someone to love is the spiritual responsibility of everyone with enough time to spare.

Marriage should serve as an incentive to develop unconditional love.

The good news about the person in the story above was her active involvement in volunteering for causes that helped others in need. During her spare time, she became engaged in helping senior citizens who lived alone and had no family around. Soon she became linked to a woman in her mid-90s, developing a very close grandmother-granddaughter relationship that became a positive force in both their lives. The single adult found so much satisfaction in helping the older woman that her disposition radiated kindness and joy. Remarkably, her optimistic bearing became so evident that she attracted the attention of a young man she knew who had never exhibited any special interest in her until now. A few months later they became engaged and were subsequently married.

Being in an intimate relationship, such as marriage, should serve as an incentive to help us develop unconditional love. This is the kind of life God envisions for everyone who wants to be His disciple. After all, a woman or man who is filled with the Spirit of God will spontaneously produce the results of love, which will radiate to those around them. That love, according to the apostle Paul's Spirit-led message, is accompanied by joy, peace, longsuffering, kindness, goodness, faithfulness, gentleness and self-control.

We pray that this will be your experience today and every day, for the rest of your life, as you invite God's Spirit into your life each day.

Pause

Is your marriage governed by rules, or by grace? Or do you need both for a happy and healthy marriage? The fruit of the Spirit is not a set of rules – it cannot be commanded. How does this work in your marriage? Talk about these serious matters in a fun and non-threatening way.

Pray

The fruit of the Spirit is the result of Christ living in us (Galatians 2:20). Pray for Christ to take full control of our lives.

Choose

Marriage is not all about us. What can we do this week to exhibit the fruit of the Spirit to those beyond our family?

Loving Like Christ

'Husbands, love your wives, just as Christ also loved the church and gave Himself for her.' Ephesians 5:25

After many years of working with couples, we have noticed that premarital couples tend to be idealistic, while married couples are often pessimistic.

Premarital couples are more likely to express how much they really love each other; the realities that we are sharing with them do not apply, so the problems others have faced will not touch them. They are ready for life together for the rest of their lives. In fact, they can't wait to spend every possible waking moment with each other. After all, they are soul mates.

On the other hand, married couples who have faced many realities of married life are often more likely to be a little jaded. It isn't that you don't love your husband or your wife: you are merely put off by their eccentricities and are not very sure whether any of this can actually change. So, when we work with marrieds, we often find them unmotivated and tired of feeling that their expectations for marriage will never truly materialise.

What makes marriage possible is that we are called to love each other as Christ loves us.

The verse for today in Ephesians 5:25 finds the apostle Paul writing a letter from prison in Rome to the believers in Ephesus – a city in Asia Minor – in today's Izmir Province of Turkey, where he ministered for some three years. Here Paul spells out to us what it means to live out the Christian life in community. The apostle advances that, after all God has done in Christ to redeem us and to make us His church, we should behave towards one another in a way that honours Him.

Indeed, whether your outlook on marriage is idealistic or pessimistic, what makes marriage possible is that, as members of the church of the God of heaven, we are called to love each other as Christ loves us. If idealistic when you got married, realism takes over soon enough, in that we are all sinners and will make mistakes. Still, we are called to live in marriage as God deals with His imperfect church.

While wives are called to submit (vs. 22), husbands are called to love their wives as Christ loved the church and gave Himself for her. This type of love is patient, kind, forgiving, and unconditional. Today we claim this kind of marriage for you as you rise above idealism or pessimism, and purpose to live as a child of God.

Pause

Routine and good habits are important for personal and emotional stability; but they can also become fossilised, and an irritant to your spouse. In a spirit of self-deprecation and humour, talk together about your own foibles.

Pray

Of the serious habits raised that irritate your spouse, listen carefully with an open heart to what they are saying, and if necessary request that the Lord help each of you change, for the benefit of each other.

Choose

If change is necessary, decide this week to deal with one small habit that irritates. Overcoming a habit is not easy, particularly one that perhaps is lifelong. Seek help and understanding from both the Lord and your spouse as you begin this journey.

....

....

....

....

....

....

....

....

....

....

....

Altruistic Love

'Let nothing be done through selfish ambition or conceit, but in lowliness of mind let each esteem others better than himself.'
Philippians 2:3

Marriage can be the most wonderful relationship in which to be, or the most difficult, depending on how you do relationships. How you feel about your partner – whether you keep a scorecard of how much you do vis-à-vis how much your spouse does in the marriage – will determine your level of satisfaction.

We've often heard people say to married friends: 'You have to make sure you are not taken for granted by your mate'; or, 'Don't do too much for her'; or, 'Don't do too much for him because he will never pull his own weight in your marriage.'

While we are not advocating for anyone to be allowed to be treated like a doormat in their marriage, we are suggesting that everyone should take responsibility for not making their marriage more difficult than it needs to be. To be sure, the most predictable, reliable, and unavoidable way to experience ongoing frustration in your marriage is to approach it from the perspective of how much you can get, rather than how much you can give. This is looking at your marriage through the proverbial glass that is half empty, rather than seeing it as a glass that is half full.

Keeping score will not enhance the quality of your relationship.

For a number of reasons, it appears irresistible to keep score either silently or out loud about how much you sacrifice for your marriage and all you do to make your marriage what it is. Talking about how many days in a row you have picked up the children from school, given them baths and put them to bed, or how many times you have done the laundry in the last month, may make you feel superior in your marriage. However, it will not enhance the quality of your relationship.

Allowing yourself to think this way may easily lead you down a path of anger, resentment, anxiety, tension and trauma. If you feel this way, your spouse will pick up your antipathy and internalise discouraging feelings about your relationship, leading him or her also to feel taken for granted in the relationship.

That is why we should 'let nothing be done through selfish ambition or conceit'. When you focus on altruistic love – what you can give, rather than what you can get – your marriage will experience the joy, grace and blessings God wants you to have.

Make this your effort today.

Pause

What if God chose to keep a scorecard rating on us? Privately consider what His score would be for you if He were to measure it against your deeds and actions over the last seven days, at home, at work, at church and at play. Because of His grace, mercy and sacrifice, the scorecard is void!

Pray

Thank God for His grace and mercy to you personally. In Philippians 2:5 (Message) Paul encourages his readers, 'Think of yourselves the way Christ Jesus thought of himself.' Pray for a mind and heart that is Christlike.

Choose

Compliment, compliment, compliment each other: not only verbally, but in as many different creative ways as possible. While it may seem a little artificial at first – particularly following a spirit of competitiveness and criticism – given time and practice, it will feel more natural.

....

....

....

....

....

....

....

....

....

....

Peace that Passes Understanding

> *'Be anxious for nothing, but in everything by prayer and
> supplication, with thanksgiving, let your requests be made
> known to God; and the peace of God, which surpasses all
> understanding, will guard your hearts and minds
> through Christ Jesus.'* Philippians 4:6, 7

Have you ever felt anxious about your job, other
concerns, or your marriage? If your answer is yes, you
need to know that anxiety is not an uncommon
occurrence, so you are not alone. In fact, millions of
people around the world – including persons in the
most developed and affluent countries of the world –
experience this sometimes very debilitating emotion.

Sharing with you that there are others experiencing
similar sensations, of course, is of little
comfort unless there is help available. In
times of anxiety and great concern we
need to know that there is something or
someone who can make a difference in
our present reality to turn things around.
At the very least, we need a measure of
assurance that our mountain of a
problem can be greatly reduced to
manageable bits.

*God always
knows what is
best, and He
can be trusted.*

The truth is, your job may not be saved during the
cuts at your place of employment. Also, worrying about
how to improve your marriage may not be quickly
resolved unless you find the right professional to help
you. Despite these realities, it is essential to arrive at a
place of calm and comfort. Truly, even if the
predicaments have not yet been totally unscrambled or

sorted out, you want to realise a measure of well-being and solace.

So how can you achieve this level of equilibrium? Glad you asked. This is precisely where Paul's message of peace finds its greatest application, because this sense of serenity and tranquillity does not emanate from thin air. The assurance spoken about here comes from praying: however, not the quick, frivolous invocation we often employ when in need of something from God, or when we are in a hurry for something to happen. The plea spoken about here is one that comes from a person who loves God and honours Him by putting their trust in God. The supplication mentioned in the text represents the earnest, sincere, and heartfelt desire of a sinner in need of assistance.

When there is a genuine and intimate relationship with God, you can present your concerns with calm assurance, realising that He knows what is best and can be trusted. You can actually thank God even before your requests are granted, knowing that, regardless of what transpires, He is near and He cares.

We pray that, regardless of your circumstances, you will make this your experience today.

Pause

'God whispers to us in our pleasures, speaks in our conscience, but shouts in our pains.' (C. S. Lewis.)

In the context of your marriage journey, experiencing life's ups and downs, how has prayer helped you both? When has God whispered? When has He spoken? When has He shouted?

Pray

Read together again Philippians 4:6, 7 as a prayer, requesting what God offers for your personal and married life.

Choose

This week:

'Keep your wants, your joys, your sorrows, your cares, and your fears before God. You cannot burden Him; you cannot weary Him. He who numbers the hairs of your head is not indifferent to the wants of His children.' (Ellen G. White, Steps to Christ, *p. 100.)*

Yes, You Can

'I can do all things through Christ who strengthens me.'
Philippians 4:13

Every married person will sooner or later experience feelings of doubt, misgiving and uncertainty about their marriage. You may have questions about whether you made the right choice. You may wonder if you should have waited longer before getting married; or you may now think your parents were right when they encouraged you to make a different choice.

Despite the emotions you may be dealing with right now, you have the capacity to employ a different outlook. Quite frequently, married people tend to assign motives to their spouse that are far from what is really taking place.

You can develop a 'can do' attitude.

We have come to the place where we realise that to a great extent our marriage will be what we choose for it to be. How is that, you may ask? After all, you can't control what your partner will do or say. And you are correct about that. However, each person has the capacity not only to control their response, but to put a positive spin on the interaction they've just had with their spouse.

While it is true that 'spin' has negative connotations, especially in politics, what we are proposing is completely different to trying to deceive others or deceive ourselves about what is happening in our marriage. We believe that looking at a situation from a positive perspective – again, the glass that is half full, rather than the negative view of the glass that is half empty – will put us in a better place and frame of mind to deal with the less-than-ideal situation at hand.

You can choose whether to develop a 'can do' attitude, knowing that with God on your side you can do anything, or whether to embrace a pessimistic perspective that will undeniably destroy your marriage. Instead of thinking, *I always have to make our bed*, you can reason, *I get to make our bed*. One is a burden, the other a privilege.

Of course, this doesn't mean you will never raise issues that you are uncomfortable with or ask to have conversations about behavioural patterns that are harmful to your relationship. What it does mean, though, is that you can choose to give your partner the benefit of the doubt, rather than ascribing a negative motive to everything your spouse does.

We hope you will remember today that you can do all things through Christ, who promises to employ His strength on your behalf.

Pause

Who does what in your household? Are the chores shared equally, or do some fall more on one spouse than the other? Is the loading fair? In days gone by, one spouse used to be the wage-earner; the other, the homemaker. Do we have realistic expectations of each other? Discuss this together.

Pray

Pray for Christ's spirit of generosity to all. 'For God so loved the world that He gave . . .' (John 3:16). Pray for the ability to generously 'give' to each other.

Choose

Is it time to introduce some changes to the way the home is run? For example, does your spouse always do the cooking? Surprise him or her by taking the initiative to take on a household task that you do not usually do. Expect to find compliments flying everywhere!

He Will Supply

'And my God shall supply all your need according to His riches in glory by Christ Jesus.' Philippians 4:19

Several years ago, we presented a family effectiveness workshop at a leadership conference for institutional leaders. In the process of sharing skills about navigating the inevitable challenges relationships often produce, the issue of patience emerged. The conversation that ensued was incredibly fascinating.

One of the leaders at the conference mentioned above exclaimed: 'My work is very intense, multifaceted, and time-sensitive.' He went on to say: 'My wife moves very slowly and challenges my capacity to do my work well. Don't you think I have the right to expect her to move more quickly?'

'Well,' we said, 'the only time patience is needed is when you are in a hurry. If there is no rush, then there is no reason to be patient.'

When it comes to marriage, because it is the closest relationship most adults will have, you can anticipate conflicts. This is the natural result of having two individuals who share the same living space and most times have very different opinions about life. Of course, the opposite usually happens when you are dating or courting. During this period, both men and women tend to be on their best behaviour, often going overboard to please each other, hoping to get to marriage. Once married, however, each is inclined to become more

Believe that God can take care of your lack of patience today.

protective of their feelings and ideas, leading to disagreements, arguments and despair.

So, we are back to the virtue of patience, defined by *Dictionary.com* as 'the quality of being patient, as the bearing of provocation, annoyance, misfortune, or pain, without complaint, loss of temper, irritation, or the like'; also, 'an ability or willingness to suppress restlessness or annoyance when confronted with delay: to have patience with a slow learner'.

We know how easy it is to agonise over our weaknesses, especially when dealing with gaps in skills that can help us have a more effective marriage relationship. As Paul says in Romans 7:15, 'For what I will to do, that I do not practice; but what I hate, that I do.' It is the very reason the apostle later offers the text for today. Paul is at peace about his personal needs, knowing that God has promised to supply them. You too must believe that your lack of patience, which is preventing you from having the best possible relationship with your spouse, is something that God can take care of today. Accept this promise by faith, and receive God's strength to experience the best time of your life in marriage today.

Pause

Waiting is a discipline, particularly in the context of relationship change. As the saying goes, 'Old habits die hard.' For the moment, remember the times when you were on your best behaviour while dating or courting. Laugh together about those happy times.

Pray

As you pray for patience with each other, pray for the Lord's help, remembering that with Him there are three people in your marriage, and He is the Mighty Counsellor!

Choose

There's no point in just talking about those happy times dating and courting. This week, use your creativity to try reliving them. Yes, go on a date together – but best behaviour is a must!

The Power of Pausing

'*My dear brothers and sisters, take note of this:*
everyone should be quick to listen,
slow to speak and slow to become angry.' James 1:19 (NIVUK)

One of the most challenging realities in relationships, especially in marriage, is having the capacity to communicate effectively. What makes accomplishing this assignment so difficult is that as human beings – sinners – we are all nursing hurts from the past and are constantly in a mode of self-protection.

Practise active listening regularly for effective communication.

This state of affairs has been the case since Adam and Eve sinned in the Garden of Eden and went into hiding from God. In Genesis 3:12, when God finally finds Adam, he defends himself by blaming Eve. In Genesis 3:13, Eve blames the serpent; and humans have been protecting themselves ever since by the way they interact with each other in their relationships.

Most children learn to behave in certain patterns based on the way they were conditioned in their families of origin. These habits, fortunately or unfortunately, have not necessarily been consciously embraced by individuals. Rather, they have been passed down through generations, becoming instinctively the default behaviour exhibited in adult life.

So, unless our parents or significant adults in our lives who reared us modelled effective communication on a regular basis – most humans haven't had this experience – the chances are that our first misunderstanding in marriage didn't work out so well (we know; we've been there): and we probably blamed our spouse for their bad attitude and the reason our conversation went so poorly.

A sensible perspective would suggest that couples need to learn and regularly practise active listening in order to develop more effective communication styles. Of course, this would enhance their relationship and build a stronger and healthier marriage. It is the reason why we often tell couples that when their partner says something they don't like, instead of being reactive by responding in a way that will escalate the conversation, they should create a space before responding.

Now, in the space that has been created, we counsel couples to practise three skills before responding: first, pause/pray. This is a quick pause to catch your breath, calm yourself down and send up a silent prayer for help. Then, think about what you should not say and what you should say to keep your relationship strong. And, finally, choose the right thing to say to keep your marriage moving in the right direction.

This is truly the message James offers here: so trust Jesus to give you the power to be patient and pause at the right time in all your conversations today.

Pause

As you communicate with each other, is one a listener and the other an interrupter? Or do you both at times, albeit unintentionally, talk over each other? Take time to reflect on how you communicate with each other. What are your strengths? What are your growth areas?

Pray

'Lord, as we listen to You, help us to listen to each other attentively. Help us to choose our words carefully and with sensitivity as we talk with each other. At the same time, help us to mean what we say, and say what we mean. Amen.'

Choose

Practise the principle of 'pause, pray, think, choose'.

....

....

....

....

....

....

....

....

....

....

....

....

Commitment

'And you will seek Me and find Me, when you search for Me with all your heart.' Jeremiah 29:13

Have you ever felt lost or been literally lost? If you have, you know that it is among the oddest feelings to deal with and process. For sure, being lost is not a good feeling. We know. We've been there.

It was a night in Venice, Italy, at the end of a very long and intense five-week work itinerary. Being far away from the experience now and having the opportunity to think about the episode, we can easily note that our exhaustion did not help our sense of direction or capacity to focus well.

We had spent two weeks in Manila, conducting leadership training in marriage enrichment for the Southern Asia-Pacific Division, speaking for government agencies during the day and for a family evangelistic series at the Pasay church in the evening. At the end of our time in the Philippines we boarded a flight at the Ninoy Aquino International Airport in Manila, on our way to Venice. Following a train ride down the Adriatic Coast to Rimini, we spoke for several days in the town of Torre Pedrera for an Inter-Ministries Convention of the Inter-European Division. To compound our tiredness, we next travelled by train to Florence, where we lectured for several days to theology students at Villa Aurora – the Adventist seminary in Tuscany – and trained several pastors to work with premarital and

If you search for God with all your heart, you will find Him.

marital couples. Later, we caught a train back to Venice, where we would board a flight home to Washington, DC.

It was late afternoon by the time we arrived in Venice. In fact, it was just a few minutes away from sunset. Our better senses argued that we should go to sleep and wake up refreshed for the flight home; but our romantic senses reasoned that we could not pass up such an exceptional opportunity to enjoy an evening in Venice: perhaps a scrumptious Italian dinner, a gelato near the Rialto, and a quick visit to St Mark's Square. Two hours later, after taking a wrong turn in the cold and drizzly night where we spent anxious moments hoping to survive the ordeal, we finally found a water bus that took us to more familiar territory and to a memorable evening in Venice.

There will be times when you will feel lost in your marriage, as we did in Venice on that eventful evening. Yet, if you search for God with all your heart, you will find Him; and He will help you unscramble whatever ails your marriage and bless you with a remarkable life.

Pause

Who expects marriage on the 3,650th day to have the same sparkle as on the 36th? By day 3,650 parenting could be the major agenda item. Add to that the financial reality that both Mum and Dad need to work outside the home. Why not take a step back and a deep breath, and let out a long sigh – together, but with a smile on your faces?

Pray

'Lord, refresh us like only You can. We are tired; very tired. You know our daily responsibilities. You know our concerns. You know our finances. Thank You that we have You as our Guide and Counsellor. Thank You that we have each other for support. Help us to find time to enjoy the pleasure of each other's company in this beautiful but challenging life stage. Amen.'

Choose

If you are at the life stage with children or teenagers, certain times need scheduling for 'us' time. Plan for a friend to child-mind to give you time and space for each other.

....

....

....

....

....

....

....

....

....

....

The Perfect Wedding

'Then God said, "Let Us make man in Our image, according to Our likeness; let them have dominion over the fish of the sea, over the birds of the air, and over the cattle, over all the earth and over every creeping thing that creeps on the earth." So God created man in His own image; in the image of God He created him; male and female He created them. Then God blessed them.'
Genesis 1:26-28

Weddings are such joyous occasions. At the same time, they require considerable coordination and planning. For this reason, many brides and grooms today seek the assistance of a wedding planner to help them navigate the vendors, venues, and timelines required to host this auspicious event. Contemporary wedding planners boast of their ability to help couples plan the wedding of their dreams. For that, some couples are willing to pay the hefty fees to have their dreams come true.

Your marriage is designed to be a picture of the character of God.

Imagine having your wedding planned by the Divine Designer? Truly, any wedding planned by God is designed to begin the journey of a marriage that lasts a lifetime and reflects His image.

In Genesis 1:26, God said, 'Let Us make man in Our image, according to Our likeness; let them have dominion over the fish of the sea, over the birds of the air, and over the cattle, over all the earth.' Then verse 1:27 continues, 'So God created man in His own image; in the image of God He created him; male and female He created them.' What an incredible story of a perfect wedding by a perfect God: one male and one female created to reflect the image of God!

This is our first responsibility as husband and wife. Can you grasp how incredibly delightful and humbling this task is? Do you comprehend the overwhelming awesomeness that has been given to you as a married couple? God has given marriage to humankind to show off who He is. Your marriage is designed to be a picture of the character of God. Your union as husband and wife is to be a reflection of the glory of God. This notion compels us to praise God for trusting us with this incredible gift of marriage, and more personally for the gift of each other as husband and wife.

Whether you are recently married or have been for many years, thank God for giving you the honour to reflect His beauty and magnificence in your marriage: so commit today and every day to see your marriage and your spouse in the light of God's glory.

Pause

All around us we face the forces of 'un-grace'. The 'survival of the fittest' paradigm reigns. It is at work in the media, in politics and sometimes in the church. Reflect and share together how marriage to each other can magnify the beauty of the grace of the Lord Jesus Christ.

Pray

As an old gospel song says: 'Let the beauty of Jesus be seen in me.' Pray for that reality with one word changed: replace the word 'me' with 'us'.

Choose

Pray this week for marriages you are aware of that seem to be struggling, where clearly there is tension, or where one spouse inappropriately controls the other.

Butterflies and Romance

*'Love suffers long and is kind; love does not envy; love does not
parade itself, is not puffed up; does not behave rudely, does not
seek its own, is not provoked, thinks no evil; does not rejoice in
iniquity, but rejoices in the truth; bears all things, believes all
things, hopes all things, endures all things. Love never fails.'*
1 Corinthians 13:4-8

Falling in love is easy. Well, that's because what we
perceive as love is actually a feeling, albeit a very strong
attraction, pulling us towards the source of our
fascination. While our attraction may lead to a deeper,
more meaningful relationship, what we are experiencing
is really a natural chemical reaction that occurs in our
brains when we meet a special someone. We feel
butterflies in our stomach, leading us to present
ourselves in the best light possible. Soon we are walking
down the aisle, playing on the beach during our
honeymoon, and purchasing our first sofa together.

Staying in love is not so easy. This is because
real love is not a feeling. Rather, real love is
active. Love is a verb. It is based on the principle
of unconditional care and regard. If we believe
that love is a feeling, then, as with any chemical
reaction, the rush soon wears off and the feelings
wane. The good news is that we can stay in love
and have romance too, but only as we have an
understanding of what true love is.

*Real love
is not a
feeling –
it's active.*

Based on our text for today, true love is not based on
experiences or gifts received. While these may
contribute to a satisfying relationship, true love is based
on how we are in the relationship: patient, kind and

humble. Essentially, do we love our spouse as Christ loves us?

Staying in love for a lifetime is possible if we learn to put our spouse before ourselves: love 'does not seek its own'. Our marriage relationship is to be a complementary one, without competition, boastfulness, or evil towards each other. We are to cherish, support and honour each other every day.

When you wake up each morning, think of a hundred ways you can be kind to your spouse. In fact, ask your spouse what you can do to make him or her feel loved today. Imagine trying to outdo your spouse in kindness! Undoubtedly, your husband or wife will feel those butterflies again. Now that's what we call real love and romance!

Pause

The core question to reflect on this week is: 'Do we love our spouse as Christ loves us?'

Share together the implications of what that means.

Pray

Thank the Lord for His great love for us. Pray that we will demonstrate in word and deed that we are His disciples, and that our spouses and others will know that we are Christians by our love.

Choose

This is kindness week. Show kindness to your spouse in every way possible.

A Forever Promise

*'Many waters cannot quench love,
nor can the floods drown it.'* Song of Solomon 8:7

Whenever we hear wedding vows couples write on their own, we are often amazed and moved by the depth of passion, emotion, and present commitment expressed in their words. Of course, what we are hearing is the current state of this couple's love for each other and what they hope for in their relationship. Wedding vows are sacred. They should represent a mutually binding commitment of love for that day and love that will last forever. Vows are a covenant agreement taken before God, family, and the community at large where you promise to love, honour, cherish and be faithful until death, regardless of the circumstances that will inevitably come your way.

Song of Solomon 8:7 describes this well by stating, 'Many waters cannot quench love, nor can the floods drown it.' Wedding vows are not just pleasant words to impress those who are listening. Rather, they are assurances of a commitment meant to last a lifetime. They represent a promise that will go beyond the wedding day and bring hope for a secure future together as a couple.

Our promise to our spouse gives our marriage a stable identity.

Wedding vows are not a guarantee that married life will always be blissful. However, they are meant to lay a foundation to hold the couple accountable when challenges arise.

There is much research that reveals that two thirds of

unhappy marriages can become happy if the partners stay together and work on their marriage. What makes the difference with those who stay married? They keep the promise of their vows and remind themselves that they made a pledge before God, their family and their friends.

Our vows keep us in the marriage even when we experience temporary unhappiness or don't feel satisfied with the marriage. They encourage us to seek solutions that will restore our love for each other and work out our differences. Our promise to our spouse gives our marriage a stable identity. It reminds us that we are an *us*, not an *I*. To be sure, when we make marriage vows, we develop a new identity as a couple.

Make the time today to take a new look at your marriage vows. If you can't find them, write new ones or adapt someone else's. Remind yourself of how you felt on your wedding day, and begin doing the things that you did in those early days that expressed your love to your spouse. These small acts of loving behaviour will lead to restoring the feelings of love you experienced when you made that forever promise.

Pause

What does it mean when Christians believe that marriage is both permanent and exclusive? Discuss this together.

Pray

Pray for the Lord's help to grow together, through the power of His Holy Spirit, turning 'I' into 'us'.

Choose

Watch out for those 'I' moments this week – not in your spouse, but in you!

....

....

....

....

....

....

....

....

....

....

....

....

....

....

....

The Best and the Worst

'For you, brethren, have been called to liberty; only do not use liberty as an opportunity for the flesh, but through love serve one another. For all the law is fulfilled in one word, even in this: "You shall love your neighbor as yourself." But if you bite and devour one another, beware lest you be consumed by one another!' Galatians 5:13-15

Marriage is designed to bring out the best in us, but it also brings out the worst in us. If you're human, then you know exactly what this means. We are more likely to show our true selves to our spouse because we perceive that to be what true intimacy means: to know and to be known. Intimacy is surely the goal of every good marriage. However, it does not give us permission to be nasty to one another. In fact, marriage is designed to glorify God. Therefore, we need to be mindful of how we interact with each other, even in the most difficult of circumstances.

Only through the power of Jesus Christ are we able to truly love one another in marriage.

The truth is, we all bring relationship patterns from our family of origin or previous relationships that often dictate how we relate to our spouse. We desire intimacy, yet at the same time we fear being hurt. Usually, when spouses hurt each other, it is because of their desire to protect themselves or it is motivated by selfishness. When we relate to one another in such negative ways, it creates barriers to our becoming one in marriage as God intends for husbands and wives.

We have been given the opportunity in marriage to love freely and serve one another through the power of Jesus Christ. This is what our text for today is helping us to understand better.

Only through the power of Jesus Christ are we able to push past our selfish motives and truly love one another in marriage and in our other relationships. When we love in a servant-hearted way, our love is filled with kindness, patience and self-control. We defer to the needs of our spouse and are considerate of how our words and actions will affect him or her.

Intimacy is not a licence to flood our relationship with all of our warts and selfish desires. On the contrary, intimacy requires a love that actively seeks to protect the heart of the other person and function in a way that will bring honour to God.

Pray today for God to give you the strength to give your best to one another.

Pause

We are kind, want to be kind, try to be kind – because the story of Christ's life shows that that's who He is. Because we're on a journey of personal and spiritual growth, let's admit that on some days we do better than on others. Share together about the 'kindness' story. What are the marriage 'pressure points' which can sometimes make us less than kind towards each other?

Pray

In Mark 10:51 it is recorded that Jesus notices a blind person called Bartimaeus. He asks him, 'What do you want Me to do for you?' Pray for that question to be at the top of the list in your marriage.

Choose

'What do you want me to do for you?' Begin a journey this week of making this the key phrase of the week for you both.

We Are Different; We Are Alike

*'I will praise You, for I am fearfully and wonderfully made;
marvelous are Your works, and that my soul knows very well.'*
Psalm 139:14

During the dating, courtship or engagement period, couples usually discuss ways in which they are similar. Prior to marriage most couples do not discuss their differences, or they choose to ignore their differences. 'Look at us; we both absolutely love vanilla ice cream,' a couple might say. However, the chances are that one prefers chocolate ice cream, but it feels better to agree about what both enjoy. Or another couple may say: 'Isn't it grand that we both like being close to water?' But in actuality one prefers a lake by the mountains, and the other would rather be on the beach by the ocean.

When there are differences, listen to and respect the other's needs and desires.

Somewhere within the first or second year of marriage, comparable situations occur: but what was previously a similarity is now a glaring difference. And here is where many couples begin a campaign of trying to change each other into their own likeness rather than accepting and managing their differences.

Psalm 139:14 says, 'I am fearfully and wonderfully made.' Yes, we are each made in the image of God and we each bring a wonderful uniqueness to our marriage. Couples who learn to respect this uniqueness and continue to focus on ways in which they are similar rather than different continue to experience joy and satisfaction in their marriage. We can also allow the differences to help us grow as individuals and as a couple. Sometimes the areas where we are different can teach us to be flexible and enjoy new experiences with each other.

Marriage is about growing together as a couple and glorifying God in the process. In our Christian walk, we learn how to humble ourselves and to push past our own selfishness and self-centredness to become true disciples. God expects us to do the same in our marriage. In Christian marriage, spouses learn to express themselves in an open and caring manner in humility. When there are differences, we listen to and respect the other person's needs and desires. Then we work together as a team to find solutions that respect and value each other's opinions.

So, if one of you likes vanilla ice cream and the other prefers chocolate, buy two different pints instead of a gallon of one flavour. If one prefers the mountains and the other prefers the ocean, then take turns every year, submitting to one another's desires.

Pray and ask God today to help you make shared give-and-take decisions that will enhance your marriage and glorify Him.

Pause

Between each other, do you experience 'low' or 'high' trust? Are you open and transparent with each other in all matters? Is problem solving easy or difficult? The answer to this question will be determined by how you answered the first two. Discuss.

Pray

Pray that the Lord will help each spouse to be open and transparent with the other.

Choose

Check this week that you are both truly working together as a team in three areas of your life: 1. the family finances, 2. parenting (if you have children), and 3. putting God first in your life.

Cherish One Another

'Keep me as the apple of Your eye;
hide me under the shadow of Your wings.' Psalm 17:8

Some time ago we received a very special gift from colleagues we were leaving behind as we transitioned to a new ministry assignment. It was a crystal apple from a very exquisite store, the apple being a symbol of our beloved New York City where we had spent many years of our lives and ministry. This precious gift came packaged in a turquoise blue box tied with a white ribbon and bow on top, and was placed in a matching turquoise blue gift bag.

More than two decades later, after three moves, this gift remains intact. Before every move we re-wrap the crystal apple in its original tissue paper, place it back in the pretty turquoise blue box, re-tie the pretty white ribbon into a bow around the box, and then place the box into the turquoise blue bag. This precious cargo always travels with us in the car and never in the moving van.

To cherish is like the cherry on top of loving.

It is obvious that this crystal apple is very special to us. We have cherished it all these years and plan to do so for many years to come. This is what it looks like when we cherish something special. In much the same way, we need to cherish our spouse. When we cherish something, we take extra care with it, we give it special attention, we protect it, we take time with it, and we go the extra mile for it. The way we treat something conveys whether we value it or are indifferent about it.

When we took our marriage vows, we promised to love and cherish each other. To cherish is like the cherry on top of loving. It includes soft tones, tender touches, genuine interest in the other, warmth and affection. When we cherish our spouse, we show appreciation for them, we are excited to see them succeed, we want to empower them to be their best self, and we seek to build their marital self-esteem.

Cherishing pushes beyond loving and makes it even sweeter to be in the marriage. It gives you the sense of feeling loved, not just knowing you are loved. It makes you look forward to being in the presence of the other person and want to live together until Christ returns.

Ask God today to give you the desire and will to cherish your spouse. Find the time as a couple to discuss this concept of cherishing, and share with each other ways in which you will feel cherished in your marriage.

Pause

What is it about bringing your commitment to each other before God first that provides such incredible emotional security? How might this be different for those who make the lifestyle choice to 'live together' and be 'partners' to each other?

Pray

Pray for extended family couples, friends and neighbouring couples in your community who do not enjoy the benefit from the beauty of Christian marriage. Pray for the Lord to use your holy relationship with each other to be a shining example for them.

Choose

Find as many ways as possible to be romantic with each other this week. For the husband, it's your turn on Sunday, Tuesday, and Thursday. For the wife, it's your turn on Monday, Wednesday and Friday. And on Saturday, it's the turn of you both!

....

....

....

....

....

....

....

....

....

....

....

Affair-proofing your marriage

*'The border shall go down along the Jordan, and it shall
end at the Salt Sea. This shall be your land with
its surrounding boundaries.'* Numbers 34:12

Physical and emotional boundaries are mentioned throughout Scripture and clearly play an important role for God's people, especially with regard to land ownership. Physical and emotional boundaries are also extremely important in marriage as well. Learning to protect the boundaries of your marriage will yield enormous benefits. On the other hand, not protecting the boundaries will yield disastrous results.

We often tell couples whom we counsel, or at our marriage conferences, that we are 'jealous of each other for the other'. What we mean by that is that when we are away from one another, we communicate by our behaviour to everyone around that we are taken – we are married, not single. We can do this verbally by talking about each other to others. We also do this non-verbally by the way we carry ourselves or allow ourselves to engage in certain conversations. We protect ourselves from others and from situations that could compromise the boundaries of our marriage. We know of many marriages that have fallen apart because of compromised boundaries that appeared innocent at first but changed into emotional or physical affairs. Don't play seemingly innocent games. Many

Examine yourself honestly to see where you may need stronger boundaries.

romantic affairs take place between partners of good friends.

We want to be clear that we are not talking about setting boundaries in a controlling way that doesn't allow one another the freedom to be an individual. However, when you are married, others should know that you are not open to certain flirtatious behaviours or conversations that threaten the boundaries that are in place to protect your marriage. If your spouse makes a reasonable request for you to spend less time with a co-worker, church mate, or family friend of the opposite sex, honour their request. They may be seeing or sensing something you may have overlooked.

We encourage you to honestly examine yourself and see where you may need to strengthen the boundaries of your relationship. If you see areas where you may need stronger boundaries, pray and ask God to help you build better boundaries. If the boundaries you have in place are strong, then thank God for helping you remain faithful to your spouse in every way.

Pray today and always that God will help you to set and keep healthy boundaries and to put your spouse and marriage first (after God), at all times.

Pause

Reflect on why the Bible insists that the marriage relationship between husband and wife be permanent and exclusive. Consider further the line above, 'They may be seeing or sensing something you may have overlooked.' Could this be a reality in your relationship?

Pray

Pray the Lord's prayer, focusing on the line, 'And do not lead us into temptation, but deliver us from the evil one' (Matthew 6:13).

Choose

Commit to each other that you will never put yourself in 'danger zones', and promise to be open and transparent with each other when either senses that a boundary is in danger of being compromised: the purpose being to ensure that action is taken to ensure that the boundary is not crossed.

When the Road Gets Bumpy – Part 1

'If you ask anything in My name, I will do it.' John 14:14

For our tenth wedding anniversary we fulfilled a long-time dream by visiting the beautiful island of Maui in Hawaii. As we often do when visiting a new place, we planned an itinerary that included well-known sites as well as sites that were off the beaten path. We woke up very early one morning to take the winding road up to Haleakala, the East Maui volcano, the island's highest peak, to see a majestic sunrise.

The most desired destination in Maui was to visit the seven pools and waterfalls of Ohe'o Gulch, accessed via the scenic winding Hana Highway, known as the Road to Hana. The trip was about three hours, but was worth every minute as every turn revealed more spectacular views of picturesque waterfalls, lush greenery, beautiful tropical flowers and the most panoramic views of the island.

As suggested by our travel guidebook, we stopped at one of the scenic lookouts to get lunch and drink fresh coconut water. After several other stops to enjoy more breathtaking views, we finally arrived at Hana and made our way to the most gorgeous cascading waterfalls, each one ending in a pool of fresh water and streaming into the next until they eventually crashed into the ocean. We had enjoyed a heavenly day together and were delighted by how well we had gotten along all day, despite the long road trip.

It's important to remember that you are on the same team.

Sundown was soon to come, so we agreed that it was time to make the long trip back to our side of the island. We knew that it would be a longer trip back if we returned the way we came, so we looked at the map – yes, this was before satellite navigational systems – and identified a road that cut across the island that would slash our travel time in half.

We started down the road, but before long it turned into a bumpy dirt road with no other cars, people or anything else in sight. By now it was dark, but we continued with the hope that the map was right. After about 30 minutes we arrived at a dead end, blocked by a big fence with a sign that read, 'Private property; no trespassing.' We looked at the map, then at each other, and immediately the peaceful, joyful day began to fade away.

Just as Adam and Eve in the Garden of Eden blamed each other after they sinned, we began to bicker and blame one another as well. But then we quickly realised that we only had each other, and that it was important for us to remember that we were on the same team; so we put our heads together and tried to figure out what to do next. And immediately our bright idea was that we needed to pray for God to help us find a way out.

Pause

What is it about the blame game that makes us feel good? Can you remember an incident in your marriage when, despite all the good intentions, things went hopelessly wrong? Share the story together about what happened, the stress, and the 'way out', hopefully sharing together in a light-hearted and humorous way.

Pray

Lord, help us to work together to be problem-solvers, not problem-makers.

Choose

Find ways this week of doing tasks that encourage teamwork: for example, washing the dishes together; one washing, the other drying . . . or gardening together? And, if you really want some fun, one driving the car, and the other reading the map?

When the Road Gets Bumpy – Part 2

*'And whatever things you ask in prayer,
believing, you will receive.'* Matthew 21:22

Shortly after our prayer ended, we saw the lights of a truck pull up to the gate on the other side of the road. Al McClure, the man driving the truck, turned out to be the general manager of the pineapple plantation where we were trespassing and asked what we were doing on his property. Calmly and humbly we explained our predicament. He promptly informed us that the map we had was an old map that didn't reflect the current reality. The road we were following on the map was now a private road in the Dole Pineapple Plantation. Miraculously, however, he seemed to believe our story and proceeded to open the gate and let us drive through. Subsequently, the general manager escorted us to the mansion on the plantation, offered us a box of pineapples, and set us on the right road to our hotel.

Marriage can sometimes be like the Road to Hana and back. At times it feels heavenly, like we are having the most beautiful life. Other times it gets a little bumpy and dusty, feeling a bit like we're headed down a dark road that comes to a dead end. Therefore, we must develop a prayer life as a couple that can guide us through these ups and downs. Praying together brings us closer to each other and to God. When we pray, believing that we will receive, God hears and answers.

Protect your marriage from blame and bickering.

No matter where you find yourself in your marriage, pray to God for wisdom and discernment for your marriage. Develop a regular habit of praying together as a couple so that, when rough times come, it will be natural to turn to God in prayer. When we turn to God in prayer, we are giving our problems over to Him and trusting Him to come up with better solutions than we can for ourselves. If we earnestly pray, it also softens our hearts towards each other and helps us to respond better to our mutual needs.

Discuss together how you can work as a team to protect your marriage from blame and bickering. Develop a regular routine for praying together if you don't already have one. Begin that journey today by praying together before you get out of bed in the morning and before you go to sleep at night. Talk about how praying together can be a blessing to your marriage going forwards, and then pray together and ask God to help you draw closer to each other and closer to Him.

Pause

What prayer routine do you have together that provides a meaningful and sustainable prayer life? What steps do you both need to take to improve it? What activities in your life sometimes prevent you from finding the time to pray? Oh, and one more thing: does prayer change God – or us?

Pray

Thank God for the privilege of prayer, and that He will place in both your hearts the knowledge that prayer is as necessary, and as natural, as breathing itself.

Choose

Choose to make your prayer life creative and dynamic. There are many and various ways to pray. Here are seven:

1. *Short-sentence prayers*
2. *Prayers from Scripture: for example, the Lord's prayer; Psalm 23; John 17*
3. *Reading a passage from Scripture and then responding to it in prayer*
4. *Intercessory prayer, lifting others up before the Lord*
5. *Prayer walking together in the neighbourhood, for the neigbourhood*
6. *Prayer outside in a natural setting*
7. *Reading a book of written prayer to guide your thoughts*

First Love

'Remember therefore from where you have fallen; repent and do the first works, or else I will come to you quickly and remove your lampstand from its place – unless you repent.'
Revelation 2:5

Take a few moments together and reminisce about when you first met. For most couples, no matter where they are in their relationship, it brings a smile to their faces. Most of us remember how very in love we felt. Somehow the skies were bluer, the grass was greener, and the stars shone brighter.

The amygdala, that part of the brain that stores emotions, will bring to memory the flood of delightful feelings that we experienced in those early days. Do you still feel butterflies in your stomach when you see each other? Do you still go out of your way to open the door, or cook a nice meal, or find a great restaurant that you both enjoy? If not, where did those feelings go? Actually, those feelings didn't go anywhere. They simply need to be intentionally recreated over and over again. We must continue doing the things we did at first.

Take the time to rekindle the spark in your relationship.

Our text today is really speaking about Christ and the Church, but it certainly applies to marriage as well. Perhaps this is why marriage is used as a metaphor for God's relationship with His people. Just as our spiritual relationship will falter if we don't nurture it, so too our marriage will fail and die if we don't cultivate and cherish it.

So, commit today to go back to the first love in your marriage. Take the time to rekindle the spark in your relationship. The truth is, the longer we are together, the lazier we become in our relationship, and then we blame it on not having enough time: yet we all make time for the things that are most important to us. Thus, we encourage you today to make your relationship a priority. Even if you have children, you can set aside time every day to invest in deepening the oneness in your relationship. Ask each other open-ended questions daily that will give you insights into each other's lives: questions such as, 'What is your favourite colour?' or, 'What tie is your favourite, and why?'

In addition, do one activity on a weekly basis, such as a date night: just the two of you. This could be as simple as putting the kids to bed and playing a game, or just watching a favourite programme together, or doing anything that will bond you closer together.

We encourage you to confess to God for not making your marriage a priority, and to commit to doing things that will reignite the early sparks.

Pause

Who proposed? Where? When? How? Remind each other again of your respective feelings and emotions. Surprised? Expected? Shocked?

Pray

Give thanks again that the Lord has brought both of you together, and helped you stay together.

Choose

Is the place where you proposed to each other close by? If so, revisit it. In most cases this will probably not be possible. Instead, get out the photos which celebrate the occasion of your engagement. Show them to each other, and to your children, if applicable.

Christ-centred Covenant

'I will say of the Lord, "He is my refuge and my fortress; my God, in Him I will trust." ' Psalm 91:2

Marriage was designed by God as the foundational human relationship that helps us better understand His relationship with us. God knew we would have basic human needs that could uniquely be met through the marriage union. When these needs are met, the marriage flourishes.

At the start of most marriages, we usually try to outdo one another in meeting needs. Inevitably, just like our first parents, Adam and Eve, we become self-centred and we neglect each other. It is during these times that one or both spouses will question the viability of the marriage. However, the truth is that this questioning is based solely on feelings. If we feel good about the relationship, then we believe the relationship to be stable and satisfying. When we do not feel good about the relationship, then we think that perhaps it is time to move on, or that it was not meant to be.

Learning to truly trust God is essential for a lasting marriage.

However, our feelings are not always accurate ('the heart is deceitful above all things, and desperately wicked' – Jeremiah 17:9). It is during these times that we have to remind ourselves of the commitment we made on our wedding day to honour and cherish each other, in good times and in not-so-good times. We can choose to tell ourselves that this is just a temporary feeling; that these emotions can and will pass: but only if we choose to do so. We are not suggesting that feelings are not important. Still, we must learn not to allow our feelings to make decisions for us. It is much better to put our trust in God.

Learning to truly trust God is an essential ingredient for a lasting marriage. When we turn to God in times of trouble, we will find comfort and wisdom for our next steps. In marriage we have been given the opportunity to reflect God's glory as we relate to one another each day. Without struggles in our marriage, we will never experience the opportunity to test our faith and experience God's faithfulness. Our challenges help us to grow in our relationship with each other and with God.

Pray together about your commitment to your relationship and your commitment to making your relationship a priority. Commit to putting your trust in God individually and as a couple, and to allowing God to help you make decisions that will enhance and strengthen your marriage.

Pause

When we say to each other, 'I love you', what are we saying? Are we expressing a feeling? Are we stating a principle? Both? Discuss this together.

Pray

Lord, as our trust in You grows and matures, give us the motivation, the time, and the space to invest in each other's life for mutual support, comfort, guidance, wisdom and passion.

Choose

Find ways to involve God in your major family decision processes this week. Prayer is essential, and so is the reading of Scripture, to find guidance on His will for your lives.

Showing Compassion

'Finally, all of you be of one mind, having compassion for one another; love as brothers, be tenderhearted, be courteous; not returning evil for evil or reviling for reviling, but on the contrary blessing, knowing that you were called to this, that you may inherit a blessing.' 1 Peter 3:8, 9

Sometimes couples will tell us they believe in the old adage, *honesty is the best policy.* We completely agree that honesty is the best policy, but all truth should be spoken in love. Brutal honesty is hurtful and just plain mean. When we speak the truth, it is more than being honest. It is being kind, being compassionate, and being a great companion. In marriage, we must resist the urge to 'keep it real', as is often urged in our contemporary society. The truth does not have to be ugly, nasty or cruel.

In order for our marriage to thrive, we need to know how to communicate for maximum positive results. Too often, we allow ourselves just to say the first thing that comes to our mind, believing that we just have to get it out. However, it is really more sensible to edit your thoughts, which will lead us to words that will affirm, nurture, and safeguard the oneness in our marriage. No one needs to suffer in silence, but we just need to learn how to speak up in a kind and compassionate manner.

Be a blessing so that you may inherit a blessing.

God designed marriage to help us to grow healthy: emotionally, intellectually, spiritually, physically and even financially. If we are going to accomplish this goal, we must learn to be compassionate to one another. This text today gives an entire lesson on what it takes to have a great marriage. Love deeply. Be tenderhearted. Be polite. Be courteous. Do not retaliate. Be a blessing so that you may inherit a blessing.

Imagine how amazing your marriage would be if you each committed to being compassionate every day. Every one of us wants to feel warmth and affection. We will all thrive and flourish in such an environment. Every marriage would be as a little heaven on earth if we followed this counsel.

Ask God to show you how you can be a blessing to your spouse and show love and compassion in every interaction you have with each other. Challenge yourself to pause and think before you speak, and ask if your words will convey love, kindness and compassion.

Pause

Love, kindness and compassion cannot be made into rules; neither can the fruit of the Spirit Paul talks about in Galatians 5:22, 23. What difference would there be to your marriage if the 'fruit of the Spirit' values were a priority to be lived in each of you?

Pray

Pray for the fruit of the Spirit.

Choose

Read together stories from the gospels that show examples of the compassion of Christ.

Becoming Soul Mates

'A friend loves at all times.' Proverbs 17:17

We often ask premarital couples what attributes they would like to have in a mate. The answers are usually a good companion, an empathetic listener, loyalty, a friend with benefits, someone who is fun. Most of these are traits of a good friend. So, in essence, marriage is a friendship with benefits. Most couples start out with a good taste of friendship: but, in order for this friendship to last, or for the partners to truly become soul mates, this friendship must be cherished, cultivated and nurtured.

Deepening friendship in marriage is essentially what God intended when He said in Genesis 2:18, 'It is not good that man should be alone; I will make him a helper comparable to him.' God created the perfect friend, companion and helper for Adam, and He wants the same for us in our marriage. The female speaker in the Song of Solomon proclaims, 'This is my beloved, and this is my friend' (Song of Solomon 5:16).

Be intentional about making time to talk as friends.

Friendship in marriage grows stronger when we commit to preserving our friendship. A friend is someone we are comfortable sharing our hopes, dreams and goals with. Friends respect one another and feel accepted by each other. Friends talk about all kinds of concerns that run the gamut of their lives. Too often, couples fall into a rut of discussing only the routine matters of life such as finances, the children's schooling, and car issues, mostly problems. While these are important to discuss, if that is all they discuss with each other then they will cease to see each other as friends.

You must learn to protect your friendship from issues and problems. After all, you did not get married only to solve problems. In fact, the better your friendship is, the easier it will be to solve your problems. When couples are really serious about maintaining their friendship, they are intentional about making time just for talking as friends on a daily basis. One way to do this is to keep updating the information you have about each other. Pay attention to the small things that you each like or don't like. Do you know whether or not your spouse still likes the colour blue? Do you know what your spouse worries about or is hopeful for? Asking open-ended questions will allow for thoughtful conversations that bind you closer together.

Marriage is intended for us to know one another, not just physically, but also emotionally and spiritually; so ask God today to help you commit to getting to know your partner better each day, to become best friends and soul mates.

Pause

Is it easy to talk with your spouse about spiritual matters?

How about talking about matters dealing with emotions and feelings? Easy or difficult?

What shared interests do you most enjoy talking about?

Pray

Pray for mature spiritual and emotional intimacy, which is the outcome of a beautiful, deep and forever friendship.

Choose

Good relationships are good because they have been worked at, and they continue to require work. However, this is not work that is drudgery, but fun and joyful. What meaningful conversation could take place this week to deepen your friendship with each other?

Do Good and Pursue Peace

'He who would love life and see good days,
let him refrain his tongue from evil, and his lips from
speaking deceit. Let him turn away from evil and do good;
let him seek peace and pursue it.' 1 Peter 3:10, 11

The Bible reminds us that we are all born in sin and shaped in iniquity (Psalm 51:5). Developmental psychologists have subsequently confirmed this by explaining it as expressed needs that, if left unmet, will mould us into maladjusted individuals. Hence, we bring to our marriage strands of selfishness, family-of-origin habits and issues, gender differences, and our own preferences. All of these can damage the oneness and intimacy in our marriage as we encounter conflicts and differences that will unavoidably appear.

It is important to work hard to limit negativity.

This wonderful passage of Scripture is telling us that, if we want to enjoy life, we should watch what we say, avoid evil, and do our best to pursue peace. This leads us to believe that because of our sinful nature we will be tempted to do and say evil things, especially in marriage. As Christians, we are not exempt from temptation. In fact, we are prone to sin and selfishness. This means that we must be on the alert, being mindful and self-aware. All of the baggage we bring into marriage will trigger certain responses that will tempt us to say or do things that can cause emotional pain to our spouse and to our marriage. This is where we need to resist evil and do our best to say and do only that which will bring peace, harmony and goodwill to the relationship.

It is important to remember that none of us is perfect, and there will be times when we are not at our best. When this happens, pursuing peace means offering a sincere apology and doing everything possible to repair any damage that has been caused. It is equally as important to recognise your spouse's attempt to turn the situation around and affirm their efforts to do so. Most relationships can handle negative interactions when there are genuine attempts to remedy the harm caused. Still, it is important to work really hard at limiting all that is negative, while increasing positive interactions.

God desires our marriage and home to be a location where kindness, joy, and peace are in a prominent place. A marriage where these elements are in residence will create a climate that fosters oneness, togetherness and solidarity.

Ask God to fill you with the yearning to refrain from evil, the longing to do good and the desire to pursue peace in your marriage today.

Pause

Our marriage, our home, our family, our bed is the safest place in the world – emotionally, physically and spiritually. Discuss this sensitively together and explain why this might be and should be true.

Pray

Give thanks for the security marriage to each other offers – all aspects of it.

Choose

Your spouse is obviously your true best earthly friend. Why not plan this week a recreational activity that you both really enjoy?

....

....

....

....

....

....

....

....

....

....

....

....

....

....

Don't Touch Those Blinds

*'The fear of the L*ORD* is the instruction of wisdom,
and before honor is humility.'* Proverbs 15:33

Early in our marriage, we quickly discovered that we both had very interesting idiosyncrasies. One of these eccentricities was which way the bedroom blinds should be turned. It seems like a simple thing, right? But it wasn't. Depending on how the blinds are flipped, light comes into the room in different ways. One of us would wake up and flip the blinds up, and the other would come behind and flip the blinds down. But we would never see the other doing this blind flipping, until one day I (Elaine) saw Willie going towards the blinds and shouted, 'Don't touch those blinds!' You can just imagine what happened after that.

Who do you think is right? The truth is, we're both right. No matter what scientific support you come up with, it simply does not matter which way the blinds should be turned. What's crucial here is being wise and humble enough in these matters to respect each other's preference. In too many marriages spouses spend a lifetime trying to convince each other that their way is the right way. To be sure, if it isn't illegal, immoral, or unethical, either way could be the right way. In other words, if it is not a sin, respect one another and come up with a solution that works and shows regard for both perspectives. Perhaps you can agree that you will take turns opening the blinds, or you will turn one window blind up and another one down.

Ask God for the wisdom to humble yourself.

The key is to find a solution that does not keep you in the same loop of arguing about negligible matters.

John Gottman, a leading marriage researcher, points out that 'most marital arguments cannot be resolved. Couples spend year after year trying to change each other's mind – but it can't be done . . . because most of their disagreements are rooted in fundamental differences of lifestyle, personality, or values. By fighting over these differences, all they succeed in doing is wasting their time and harming their marriage.'[1]

If you have been trying to work on an issue that is more about your annoyance rather than a biblical principle, commit to letting it go. Ask God for the wisdom to humble yourself so you can focus more as a couple on loving each other and solving your solvable problems.

[1] John Gottman and Nan Silver, *The Seven Principles for Making Marriage Work* (Orion Spring, 2018)

Pause

How does the 'give and take' principle work in your marriage? Who seems to 'give' the most, and who seems to 'take' the most? Discuss this gently, and certainly don't get into an argument about it! Is it possible that, in this discussion, I might see something about myself that makes me uncomfortable?

Pray

Lord, am I really as my spouse describes? Help me to grow into the 'grace' leader in our marriage. Lord, help us both to commit to standing firm on important life matters, but outshine each other in generosity of spirit, particularly on everyday matters of 'give and take'.

Choose

Galatians 6:9 says, 'Let us not grow weary while doing good. . . .' Focus on the value this text is highlighting. How can this be applied in your marriage this coming week?

'Love one another with brotherly affection. Outdo one another in showing honour' (Romans 12:10, ESVUK).

....
....
....
....
....
....
....
....

My Spouse Is Better than Your Spouse

*'Let your conduct be without covetousness; be content
with such things as you have. For He Himself has said,
"I will never leave you nor forsake you." '* Hebrews 13:5

During the holidays there are innumerable car
commercials in the media displaying automobiles with
big, beautiful red bows tied around them, with messages
that claim, 'You deserve a bigger, shinier, and better
model this year.' A number of these commercials push
the envelope even further by showing one very
disappointed neighbour receiving a lawnmower while
the other one is overjoyed and jumping with excitement
over the brand-new expensive vehicle in the driveway.
Our culture encourages this pattern of craving more,
coveting what others have, which
leads to dissatisfaction, discontent
and displeasure with what we already
have. It also leads us to overlook the
many blessings we receive daily from
God.

*Learning to be
content is a
spiritual principle
and a spiritual
discipline.*

In our marriage, we have learned –
and are still learning – how to be
content with each other and with
what God has given to our family. The
truth is, there will always be other
couples who have nicer cars, bigger houses, smarter
children and classier clothes, and who enjoy more
extravagant vacations than we do. Making the choice to
be content with what you have, however, is the antidote
to discontentment, which is not the same as settling for
mediocrity. On the contrary, it pushes us to strive to

build on what we already have and make it the best it can possibly be.

Our daughter, who is now married and lives several hours away from us by car, recently told us how fondly she remembers the fun times our family had when we would go ice skating every New Year's Day. There were other swankier, more expensive skating rinks that other families visited, but this venue was free and worked well with our budget and our priorities. Guess what? It was not the rink that sparked our daughter's memory bank, but the fun and feeling of family togetherness we enjoyed. Learning to be content is a spiritual principle and a spiritual discipline.

Being content with your spouse and your marriage honours God, your marriage and your spouse. Instead of comparing your mate or your marriage to other people or unrealistic expectations from the media, stop and thank God for the blessing He has given you in your spouse. We are not suggesting that you should have a lacklustre form of contentment: rather, that you should experience an exhilarating, enrapturing (Proverbs 5:19) satisfaction with your marriage and your spouse. The choice is yours.

So, ask God to give you the aptitude and capacity to be content with your marriage and your spouse.

Pause

How are our expectations shaped by how the media (films, TV shows, and advertisements) portray family life and relationships? More often than not, they are seen as transitional. Is it possible that this media 'window' into other people's lives (whether fact or fiction) can make you feel incredibly unsettled? Is the advertisement designed to make you feel as if you need something extra? Discuss this together.

Pray

Help us, Lord, to be settled and content with what You provide us with. Thank You for providing for our needs. Thank You for bringing us together, a gift to each other. As You live in us, and we experience Your love, control our wants.

Choose

Galatians 2:20 (ESVUK): 'I have been crucified with Christ. It is no longer I who live, but Christ who lives in me. And the life I now live in the flesh I live by faith in the Son of God, who loved me and gave himself for me.' Keep this text in focus as you go through this week.

We Are On the Same Team

'Two are better than one, because they have a good reward for their labor. For if they fall, one will lift up his companion. But woe to him who is alone when he falls, for he has no one to help him up.' Ecclesiastes 4:9, 10

Any fan of soccer knows that a teammate would never knowingly drive a soccer ball into their own team's goal. That would be absolutely insane! Yet how often do we do this in our marriage? Sometimes we inadvertently or intentionally score points against each other. Did you realise that when you got married, you became a team? As such, you need to think like a team. We go from being an 'I' to being a 'we'; we who were two are now one (Mark 10:8). This is the ultimate understanding of interdependence that God intended when He designed marriage.

Many couples lack a true understanding of this interdependence and resent the notion of becoming one. In contemporary society, this idea seems limiting, restrictive and constraining, as couples begin to do and say things to proclaim their independence. It might sound like, 'It's my money; I work hard: I can buy a new pair of shoes if I want to!' 'You're not my mother; if I want to hang with the guys after work, I'll do as I please!'

Marriage is about becoming more together.

Statements such as these are assertions of independence and simply have no place in marriage. The truth is, the day you said 'I do' is the day you gave up your independence. Of course, this does not mean that you should control one another or stifle one another. However, it does mean that you have to work together as a team for the benefit of the 'we'. A new job across the country is only great if you can both agree that it works for the good of the team. Imagine the soccer player again, scoring a goal for the opposition! Couples who work as a team are able to solve problems more easily because they are looking for the mutual benefit of the relationship. It creates a sense of mutual respect, value and regard that enhances life together as a couple.

Learning to work as a team will strengthen your friendship in marriage and can be a lot of fun. When you depend on each other, you are bonded closer together as a couple and truly begin to experience what it means to become one. Marriage is about becoming more together than you can be by yourselves.

Ask God today to give you a spirit of teamwork so you can become all He meant for you to be.

Pause

Think of the best example in recent times when you worked intensively together as a team when faced with a challenge. What gift or perspective did each bring to the table that complemented the gift of the other to solve the problem?

Pray

Thank the Lord for the team spirit in your marriage.

Choose

What skills can we develop that will help us sharpen our teambuilding skills?

....

....

....

....

....

....

....

....

....

....

....

....

....

....

What Not to Do in Marriage

'Judge not, and you shall not be judged. Condemn not, and you shall not be condemned. Forgive, and you will be forgiven.'
Luke 6:37

The story of King David and Michal, the daughter of Saul, is an epic romance with all the elements of a big feature film (see the book of 1 Samuel). There is love, passion, jealousy, separation, in-law issues; you name it: it is in this story. Nonetheless, David and Michal are the perfect example of what not to do if you want to have a stable and happy marriage.

The most poignant element found in this marriage is their contempt for each other. Apparently, at the beginning of their relationship there was some aspect of love and passion between the two; but their relationship was fraught with a lot of baggage from both sides, creating a lack of trust in their relationship, which left them disenchanted with each other and consequently with their marriage.

Accept the fact that your spouse is not perfect, and neither are you.

What exactly is contempt? A definition of contempt in *Dictionary.com* is: 'the feeling with which a person regards anything considered mean, vile, or worthless; disdain; scorn'. Those who are at the receiving end of contempt are subject to awful consequences, including experiencing shame and rejection and a diminished self-esteem. In the marital context, contempt is the biggest predictor of distress and divorce. Contempt is associated with envy, anger, and false pride. The person who shows contempt is often emotionally fragile and likely to suffer from low self-esteem.

Sometimes, contempt shows up when we feel that our standards are not being met and we feel frustrated that things are not exactly the way we perceive they should be. Psychologists believe we show contempt or demean another as a way to regain our equilibrium because we may assume that the other person is purposefully trying not to do things the way we want them done. Or we may inadvertently show contempt, believing that we are just trying to help the other person recognise their flaws and become a better person. All of these attempts are demeaning and destructive to your spouse and to your marriage.

The best way to offset contempt is to show compassion for your spouse. Accept the fact that your spouse is not perfect, and neither are you. Look for ways to affirm the positive and find the right time to discuss things that frustrate you; always use 'I' statements and resist the urge to put down your spouse.

Pray for God to help you see your spouse through His eyes, and that your spouse will see you through God's eyes.

Pause

As you communicate with each other, are you able to do so without the fear of being 'put down' by each other?

Pray

Pray for the Lord to give you both a gentle spirit.

Choose

One definition of grace goes like this: 'Grace is love that stoops – and cares – and rescues.' How will this work in your marriage this week?

....

....

....

....

....

....

....

....

....

....

....

....

....

....

Fifty Years from Now

'Be of good courage, and He shall strengthen your heart, all you who hope in the LORD.' Psalm 31:24

Andy Denton, a musical artist, sings a song titled, 'Fifty Years from Now'. It is one of our favourite songs because it sums up the cycle of married life. The song begins by asking, 'What do you do when the fire is gone and the passion fades to grey?' Then the chorus asks, 'Fifty years from now, what will you remember?' Will you remember those early dates, your wedding day, your children's music recitals and sports activities, graduations, birthday parties? Or will you throw out all these memories?

It is a powerful reminder that sometimes we focus more on the negative aspects of our relationship and forget all the positive experiences we have had and can continue to have. When people ask us how we have managed to stay married for thirty-five years, we say we are looking forward to celebrating our fiftieth wedding anniversary. We have committed to nurturing the long-term view in our marriage and keeping that hope alive.

'What do you do when the fire is gone and the passion fades to grey?'

Couples must develop the habit of thinking positively about the future of their marriage. In contemporary society, the tendency is to think about divorce or separation as soon as there are significant problems in the relationship. We are being conditioned to believe that if there is any stress, discomfort or tension, then the marriage is doomed. In our work, however, we have met many couples who have gotten divorced, not because of infidelity or abuse, but because they simply were not getting along. The sad part is that many of these couples are willing to put in the time preparing for marathons or golf tournaments, learning to knit, sew or crochet, or completing their educational and career goals. While all of these are remarkable pursuits, if we employed some of this energy in our marriage, we would actually have a great marriage.

As Christians, while we may not be able to see what the end looks like, especially during difficult times, we can trust God to see it for us. In marriage, when we keep an eternal perspective of hope, it helps us to think more positively about our relationship: yet, if we continue to cultivate a dismal picture of our marriage, it will lead to hopelessness and despair.

So, ask God today to help you to be of good courage and keep hope alive in your marriage.

Pause

What do you think of the statement made on the previous page?

'While all of these are remarkable pursuits, if we employed some of this energy in our marriage, we would actually have a great marriage.'

Discuss this together.

Pray

Lord, in each of us there is the desire to achieve. Thank You for putting that in our hearts. At the same time, guide us to want to achieve what is really important – and lasting.

Choose

One critical lack of 'marriage investment' is time. How is your work-life balance? Are you such a busy couple that you never have time for each other? And even if you do, are you so overcome with tiredness that nothing recreationally meaningful happens? This week, find time to do a simple time-management audit.

Becoming a Servant

'Humble yourselves in the sight of the Lord, and He will lift you up.' James 4:10

On a recent trip to the grocery store we overheard a couple chatting with each other. As counsellors, our ears naturally prick up when we see or hear couples interacting. It was a few nights before Thanksgiving (a national celebration in the United States of America), and the grocery store was crowded. This caused many couples to become agitated with the long queues, and also to become frustrated at the process and with each other. However, this couple seemed unruffled by the chaos in the store.

We heard the husband ask his wife in a very gentle and tender voice, 'Do you think we should get more cheese squares? You know, it's easy for people to take and put on their plates.' The wife then responded in an equally soft and gentle manner, 'I'm tempted to get more, but I really believe that, as we are trying to be healthier, we should serve healthier options.' At this point we snuck a peek at them in time to see the husband hug his wife and say, 'OK, Sweetheart.'

Imagine how much sweeter your marriage would be if you followed Christ's example of humility.

What intrigued us about the exchange between this couple was how gentle and kind they were with each other, deferring to one another throughout, as if trying not to step on each other's toes. We sensed that they were really trying hard not to hurt each other's feelings in their responses, but also determined to show kindness and affection as they spoke.

This is what humility in marriage looks like. It is an intentional desire and commitment to defer to one another. There was no impatience in either one of their voices, even though there could have been. It was evident that they had already discussed what they were going to purchase. The wife, though, showed no annoyance or contempt that her husband was changing his mind, and didn't make him feel dumb for asking the question. He, on the other hand, obviously made a decision to respect their earlier decision, or maybe even her decision, to eat healthier, and readily conceded.

One of the biggest issues we have to contend with in marriage is self-centredness. From the time of our birth, during our childhood and into adulthood, human beings are preoccupied with their own needs. Imagine how much sweeter your marriage would be if you followed Christ's example of humility (Philippians 2:5-8) and determined to humble yourself before God and your partner.

Ask God today to take you from being self-centred to being altruistic in your marriage.

Pause

Let's return for a moment to that shopping trip experience. Read about it again, and note how a good suggestion was refused for another, higher reason. Note the gentle spirit – almost always likely in a 'high trust' environment, of which marriage and the family should be the highest human example. Discuss this together.

Pray

Lord, because we have such a high trust in You, create in us 'high trust' in each other.

Choose

Keep close to hand this week Philippians 2:5-8. Read it to each other daily, perhaps using different Bible translations; and, for extra fun, try reciting it to each other from memory.

Keeping Your Sex Life Vibrant

*'Therefore, **whether you eat or drink, or whatever you do,
do all to the glory of God.'** 1 Corinthians 10:31*

We often get asked by married couples what they can do to keep their sex life vibrant. The easy answer, of course, is to keep their marriage alive and exciting: although the answer is usually more multifaceted than that.

Marriage often happens at the high point of two or three years of a love relationship, when the persons in the relationship feel they cannot live without each other. This process ordinarily begins with a literal high when neurotransmitters like dopamine, norepinephrine and serotonin – naturally produced by the human body – get dumped into the limbic system of the brain, triggering warm, fuzzy and in-love feelings, when two persons meet and find each other attractive.

Like all chemical highs, this one will also eventually come down. You can see it happen when people who are getting to know each other discover a habit they dislike in the other person, often leading to the termination of the relationship.

'Find out what your spouse likes and do it.'

Of course, individuals whose relationships have been able to sustain a healthy level of attraction often become married. Once married, however, partners grow familiar with each other, get into routines, and in the process of living this closely to each other are very likely to discover additional flaws in their loved one. This reality often leads to a diminished level of attraction and interest, unless they deal with the issue to the satisfaction of all.

During the honeymoon period, which extends into early marriage, lovemaking tends to be intense and pleasurable, and the partners seem not to be able to get enough of each other. This stage, to be sure, is when couples are experiencing what would be considered a vibrant sex life. And while this can be sustained for a long time if couples invest time and effort to make their relationship satisfying, eventually it will slow down as a natural part of the ageing process.

This is the reason we often say to couples: 'Find out what your spouse likes and do it.' The other half of that statement is just as important: 'Find out what your spouse doesn't like and quit doing it.'

Put these skills into practice as you ask God for help to have the kind of marriage that honours Him. After all, part and parcel of doing all things to God's glory is having a marriage filled with wonderful experiences with your spouse.

Pause

Are we able to talk about our physical intimacy (sex) in a mature, open, and non-threatening way?

Pray

Lord, help us to be real about our expectations, free of what society and convention portray, particularly through the media.

Choose

Choose whatever you think is appropriate for your circumstances and life stage, so long as it brings you closer together: not just physically, but emotionally and spiritually.

....
....
....
....
....
....
....
....
....
....
....
....
....

Marriage with a Mission

*'Hear, O Israel: The LORD our God, the LORD is one!
You shall love the LORD your God with all your heart,
with all your soul, and with all your strength. And these
words which I command you today shall be in your heart.'*
Deuteronomy 6:4-6

Mission statements are an essential aspect in every organisation. A mission statement is usually based on the values and goals of the enterprise. It reflects what we want the company to stand for and how it represents itself. So, in a similar way, God has given us very clear directives on how we can live our lives and how we can maintain our marriage with a mission.

This passage of Scripture today is part of what is called the Shema in Hebrew literature and history, and it is here that God clearly tells the children of Israel what He wants them to do in their families. By the way, this reality still applies to God's followers today. We should love Him with all our heart and all our soul. This means that everything we live for and all we do each day should be driven by this love that we have for Jehovah God. In fact, God makes very clear what our mission should be. He's telling us to listen. What, then, are we listening to? – the fact that He wants us to love Him every day, so that when we wake up our primary goal or mission is to acknowledge God's sovereignty over us and all that we do. Our sole purpose in life is to love God, which means to obey Him (John 14:15).

He's telling us to listen.

Can you imagine how transformed your marriage would be if you woke up every morning knowing that your singular mission is to love God? Can you see yourself overflowing with this love, which will give you the capacity to love like God? Can you see this love pouring into your spouse, your children or others you come in contact with?

All mission statement sages will tell you that if you are going to live by your mission, you need to put it in writing, read it several times a day and memorise it. We encourage you today to read the entire Shema, found in Deuteronomy 6:4-9, and then determine as a couple that you will pursue God's mission for your lives, individually and as a couple.

Pray to God today, and ask Him to help you have a purposeful marriage, driven by His mission.

Pause

You've burst our bubble! You mean that marriage is not all about us . . . ? Discuss and reflect on what you think God's plan is for each of you personally, and then consider how that fits into your marriage.

Pray

Lord, help us to love You with all our heart, and with all our soul, and with all our might. We pray that these words shall be on both our hearts: not only today, but always.

Choose

Keep close to hand this week Deuteronomy 6:4-9. Read it to each other daily, perhaps using different Bible translations; and, for extra fun, try reciting it to each other from memory.

Real Love

'My little children, let us not love in word or in tongue, but in deed and in truth.' 1 John 3:18

In every romantic film there are two beautiful people whose love is larger than life. Their love appears to be so real and so authentic and so much more passionate than anything we can experience in real life. Well, that is because it's not real! They are actors, and they are really good at making us believe they are in love with each other: yet, even though we know this, many still judge their real-life relationships by what they see on the screen.

Unfortunately, the notion of being in love is really based on a Hollywood portrayal of what love is; it is an outward expression that does not really permeate the inner person. Yet, while outward expression is wonderful, real love is more than flowery words and outward displays of affection. Real love is more than just looking like we are in love. Real love is loving 'in deed and in truth': and real marriage is made up of two real people who have real issues, yet are committed to doing everything possible to be truly loving.

Real love is more than flowery words and outward displays of affection.

When we present at marriage seminars, while one of us is speaking, the other one will look lovingly at the other. Afterwards, participants will tell us that they want to have a marriage just like ours. They tell us: 'We just love the way you look at each other. We can tell you are so in love!' Well, we are totally in love with each other, but, after thirty-five years of marriage, the truth is that we do not always feel very loving towards one another! So we tell couples that they can also have a great marriage – not perfect – if they are willing to weather the storms and strive to have a marriage that not only *looks* loving, but also *is* loving.

The truth is, there are many ways to have a great marriage. Your marriage does not have to look like anyone else's marriage. Too often, we see couples trying so hard to be like other couples while neglecting their own marriage. Why not write your own love story? Instead of thinking about what other couples have, focus on affirming and serving your spouse in love. We are finite human beings, but God has infinite ways in which we can learn to love like Him.

Ask God today and every day to help you not just to look like someone in love, but to truly express love to each other in words and deeds. Then watch your marriage soar beyond anything the movies have to offer.

Pause

Real love is deeper than feelings alone, and is based more on principle and commitment. Discuss this together.

Pray

Pray that your love for each other will not be shaped by Hollywood, but by the example of Christ Himself.

Choose

Marriage expresses a commitment to each other 'in sickness and in health'; and, to put it another way, through the thick and thin times of life. Remind each other with a sense of thankfulness how much you've appreciated your spouse when times have been difficult for you personally.

....

....

....

....

....

....

....

....

....

....

....

....

The Anger Cycle

'Be angry, and do not sin.' Ephesians 4:26

Psychologists have identified anger as one of several basic emotions that we experience as human beings. Emotions are not good or bad: they just help us express how we feel. Our text today reflects an understanding of anger as a human emotion. However, it cautions us that when we experience anger we should not sin. This is where many of us are challenged, especially in marriage.

A wife once wrote to us, stating that she believed she had an anger problem. She explained that her spouse was extremely critical of her, and, in order for her to protect herself against his constant criticism, she would erupt in anger towards him, sometimes even when he was not necessarily being critical. Of course, once there is a pattern of criticism, it tends to create low trust in the marriage.

Now, this wife may have had an anger problem that needed to be addressed. However, she may really just have been experiencing hurt from her husband's constant habit of putting her down or invalidating her. She may have been experiencing guilt or shame about not being able to live up to her husband's standards, so she knowingly or unknowingly used anger to hide her true emotions.

Many of us express anger in much the same way: to mask or protect our genuine emotions that lie beneath the surface. For many persons anger has become the

It is important to remember that no one can make you angry.

default emotion, because either it gets them a particular result, or very possibly they have never learned how to express any other emotion. Learning to recognise what is prompting anger in us can be very powerful for our marriage, and may allow for better understanding between spouses.

We should hasten to say here that sometimes anger can lead to physical, emotional or verbal abuse. When this happens, we strongly recommend that couples seek the help of a qualified Christian counsellor who can help them overcome this problem.

When we choose not to sin in our anger, it gives us the opportunity to consider how we can better relate to our spouse in a Christ-like manner. Ask yourself whether your tone of voice, attitude and words enhance and bless your spouse and your marriage. It is important to remember that no one can make you angry. Anger is an emotion, and you have the power to choose your emotions through the power of Christ.

Ask God today for power, determination and the will to put your anger in its proper place so that your marriage will go from good to great.

Pause

'For many persons anger has become the default emotion . . .'
– not just in the home, one might add, but in the workplace, in
politics, in the media, and even, God forbid, at times, in the
church. Do we realise what is happening to us? Are our reactions
to each other possibly shaped by how civil (or, better stated,
'uncivil') society members communicate with each other?

Pray

Lord, help us to live as the apostle Paul instructed: 'Do not be
conformed to this world, but be transformed by the renewal of
your mind, that by testing you may discern what is the will of
God, what is good and acceptable and perfect' (Romans 12:2).

Choose

Determine and continue to pray, this week and every week,
that anger will be the emotion of 'last resort' in your marriage.

Forgive and You Will Be Forgiven

'And whenever you stand praying, if you have anything against anyone, forgive him, that your Father in heaven may also forgive you your trespasses.' Mark 11:25

Chances are, if you have been married for any number of years, you have been hurt deeply by your spouse or you have deeply hurt your spouse. These hurts are inevitable in marriage, especially as spouses get to know each other more intimately; so it is vital to learn to practise the art of forgiving.

Forgiveness is an essential ingredient in marriage if we are going to experience the oneness God intends for us to have. Lewis Smedes, an acclaimed author on the topic of forgiveness, offers that: 'It is not as though forgiving were the remedy of choice among other options less effective but still useful. It is the only remedy.'

God asks us to forgive so that we can be released from our past hurts.

There are many reasons why forgiveness is the only solution for hurts that occur in marriage – or in any relationship – first and foremost, because God says that we must forgive. Our text today clearly states that if we expect to be forgiven by God for our sins, then we must forgive one another. In verse 26, we are further warned, 'But if you do not forgive, neither will your Father in heaven forgive your trespasses.' But let's be clear: God doesn't arbitrarily ask us to forgive just because He wants to make us do something. God asks us to forgive so that we can be released from our past hurts that keep us from growing closer to each other and to Him.

Forgiving your spouse does not absolve them of the wrongdoing, yet it opens the door for you to communicate about how you can have a better marriage. When we forgive, we begin to see our spouse as a frail human being, just as we are. When we forgive, we give up our right to retaliate or get even. We allow ourselves to feel empathy towards our spouse and think about restoring the closeness and warmth in our relationship. After all, it is only through God's power and grace that we are able to forgive one another; so, the sooner we push ourselves to forgive, even when we do not feel like it, the sooner our hurts will begin to heal.

Ask God to help you identify areas where you may harbour bitterness, resentment or lack of forgiveness in your marriage. Ask Him to empower you today to take steps towards forgiving your spouse for any past or existing hurts in order to bring hope and healing to your marriage.

Pause

Consider again this definition of grace, by the British pastor and evangelist, John Stott, pausing to consider what every highlighted word means in the context of the Gospel of Christ:

'Grace is love that **stoops** *– and* **cares** *– and* **rescues***.'*

Is grace a concept or a Person?
Does His love offer forgiveness?
What does it mean to stoop? (Check with a dictionary if necessary.)
What does it mean to care?
What does it mean to rescue?

Pray

Whatever the hurt, whatever the pain, whatever the sin, the Lord invites both the hurting one and the one who has hurt to turn to Him. He invites us to turn to Him, and to bring everything to Him in prayer.

Choose

Keep the definition of grace close to you personally. Reflect on it daily. How does it relate to the need to forgive your spouse, if necessary? If you are the one who has hurt, reflect on how God has forgiven you as you have confessed to Him. It may take longer for your spouse to forgive you. All the same, determine to live your life in the grace of the Lord Jesus Christ.

References

Andrews Study Bible (2010): J. L. Dybdahl, ed.), Berrien Springs, Michigan: Andrews University Press.

Carlson, R., & Carlson, K. (1999), Don't Sweat the Small Stuff in Love, New York, New York: Hyperion.

Covey, S. R. (1997), The 7 habits of highly effective families: Macmillan.

Davidson, R. M. (2007), Flame of Yahweh: Sexuality in the Old Testament, Peabody, Massachusetts: Hendrickson Publishers, Inc.

Dockery, D. S. (2011), Holman Concise Bible Commentary: B&H Publishing Group.

Doukhan, J. (2016), Seventh-day Adventist International Bible Commentary (vol. 1): Pacific Press Publishing Association.

Gottman, J. M., & Silver, N. (2015), Seven Principles for Making Marriage Work, New York, New York: Harmony Books.

Harley, W. F., Jr. (2011), His Needs, Her Needs: Building an Affair-Proof Marriage, Grand Rapids, Michigan: Revell.

Henry, M. (2008), Matthew Henry's Commentary on the Whole Bible: Hendrickson Publishers.

Keller, T. (2011), The Meaning of Marriage, New York, New York: Penguin Group.

Laaser, M., & Laaser, D. (2008), The Seven Desires of Every Heart, Grand Rapids, Michigan: Zondervan.

Mazat, A. (2001), The Intimate Marriage: Connecting with the One You Love, Hagerstown, Maryland: Review and Herald Publishing Association.

Mueller, E., & De Souza, E. B. (2015), Marriage: Biblical and Theological Aspects (E. Mueller & E. B. De Souza, eds., vol. 1), Silver Spring, Maryland: Review and Herald.

Oliver, W., & Oliver, E. (2015), Real Family Talk: Answers to Questions about Love, Marriage, and Sex, Nampa, Idaho: Pacific Press Publishing Association.

Oliver, W., & Oliver, E. (2018), Hope for Today's Families, Silver Spring, Maryland: Review and Herald.

Smedes, L. B. (1996), The Art of Forgiving, Nashville, Tennessee: Moorings Publishing.

Society, A. B. (2001), Good News Bible: American Bible Society.

Stanley, S. M. (2005), The Power of Commitment: A Guide to Active, Lifelong Love, San Francisco, California: Jossey-Bass.

Stanley, S. M., Trathen, D., McCain, S., & Bryan, B. M. (2013), A Lasting Promise: The Christian Guide to Fighting for Your Marriage: John Wiley & Sons.

White, E. G. (2001), The Adventist Home, Hagerstown, Maryland: Review and Herald.

Willie Oliver, PhD, MA, CFLE, an ordained minister, pastoral counsellor, family sociologist, and certified family life educator, is director for the Department of Family Ministries at the world headquarters of the Seventh-day Adventist Church and co-author of Hope for Today's Families.

Elaine Oliver, PhDc, MA, LCPC, CFLE, an educator, counselling psychologist, clinical mental health counsellor and certified family life educator, is associate director for the Department of Family Ministries at the world headquarters of the Seventh-day Adventist Church and co-author of Hope for Today's Families.